THE ILLUSTRATED
GOSPEL *of* MARK

N illo tempore. Reain
bentibus undeam disa
pulis apparuit illis do
minus ihesus et expiobrauit

THE ILLUSTRATED
GOSPEL *of* MARK

CHARTWELL
BOOKS, INC.

A QUARTO BOOK

Published in 2014 by
Chartwell Books, Inc.
A Division of Book Sales, Inc.
276 Fifth Avenue Suite 206
New York, New York 10001
USA

Copyright © 2014 Quarto Inc.

ISBN: 978-0-7858-3101-3

Conceived, designed, and produced by
Quarto Publishing plc
The Old Brewery
6 Blundell Street
London N7 9BH

QUA: IGSM

Editor & designer: Michelle Pickering
Proofreader: Claire Waite Brown
Indexer: Ann Barrett
Art director: Caroline Guest
Creative director: Moira Clinch
Publisher: Paul Carslake

Color separation by Cypress
Colours (HK) Ltd, Hong Kong
Printed by 1010 Printing
International Ltd, China

PAGE 1: Crucifixion of Christ (Stained-glass window in the Cathedral of St. Michael and St. Gudula in Brussels, Belgium, by Jean-Baptiste Capronnier, 19th century)
PAGE 2: Mark Writing His Gospel plus Episodes from His Life (Bedford Book of Hours, French School, c. 1423)
ABOVE: Ascension of Christ (Stained-glass panel, early 20th century)

CONTENTS

INITIVM EVANGELII IHV XPI FILII DI · SIC
SCRIPTVM EST IN ESAIA PROP · ECCE MITTO ANG

VIGILATE
ERGO NES
CITIS ENIM
QVANDO
DOMINVS
DOMVS
VENIAT
SERO
AN MEDIA
NOCTE
AN GALLI
CANTV
AN MANE
NE CVM
VENIRIT
REPENTE
VENIAT

INTRODUCTION

The New Testament of the Christian Bible begins with four books known as Gospels, written by different authors, that each describe the life of Jesus Christ. They present the Christian understanding of Jesus as the long-anticipated Jewish Messiah by describing his teachings, miracles, and resurrection.

Mark's Gospel—entitled "The Gospel According to Mark" or "The Good News According to Mark"—was the first to be written. The date of authorship is unknown, but the concern of chapter 13 with the horrors of the Sack of Jerusalem in 70 C.E. has led many to think that it was composed within a few years of that event, which was either pending in the near future or reverberating in the recent past. An early tradition links Mark with the apostle Peter, but scholars are divided about the reliability of this tradition.

In his Gospel, Mark tells the stories of Jesus that were circulating in the early Christian community. He has the brilliant artistry of an oral storyteller, with an eye for visual detail. Beginning when Jesus was about thirty years of age, with the story of Jesus' baptism by John the Baptist, the first half of Mark's Gospel is concerned with revealing to the reader who Jesus is. Mark is interested above all in the personality of Jesus and his amazing power to attract, to heal, to reconcile, and to forgive.

The turning point in the Gospel occurs in chapter 8, with Peter's recognition that Jesus was the long-awaited Messiah, or Christ. Messiah in Hebrew means "Anointed One"; Christ is derived from a Greek word of the same meaning. At the time of Jesus, the Jewish nation was a subject province in the Roman Empire. Judea, the region around Jerusalem, was ruled by a Roman governor, while the region of Galilee was overseen by a puppet king. Many Jewish people chafed under the Roman yoke and longed for relief. Hope that a Messiah would arrive to liberate them and drive out the Romans was widespread. Many charismatic leaders arose who claimed to be such a man.

Jesus was not the type of Messiah that people had expected. His message was of love and the forgiveness of sins. He proclaimed the Good News that the Kingdom of God was at hand, and that it was through his own suffering, death, and resurrection—the Passion of Christ—that he would save humanity.

The wealth of fascinating episodes in the life of Jesus as depicted in the Gospels, from the many miracles and parables to Christ's Passion and resurrection, have inspired innumerable works of art over the centuries. This book features the complete text of Mark's Gospel and is illustrated with a selection of beautiful works of art, from Old Master paintings and frescoes to stained glass and illuminations.

Mark the Evangelist

Ada School (also called the Court School of Charlemagne)
c. 800–825

This portrait of Mark is from the Harley Golden Gospels, a Carolingian illuminated manuscript produced in Germany. It is an example of Codex Aureus (Golden Books), named because of the lavish use of gold. Mark's symbol, a winged lion, is also a symbol of Venice, Italy, and his body is supposedly interred in the basilica there.

CHAPTER 1

John the Baptist predicts the coming of Jesus. When he baptizes Jesus, the Holy Spirit appears in the form of a dove and a voice from the sky calls Jesus "my beloved Son." Jesus then goes into the wilderness for forty days, where he is tempted by Satan and helped by angels. On returning to Galilee, Jesus invites his first disciples to join him as he travels around the region preaching, healing the sick, and casting out demons.

Jesus . . . was baptized by John in the Jordan. Mark 1:9

The Preaching of St. John the Baptist

Francesco Albani
1630

John the Baptist stands on the far left of the painting, wearing a leather garment around his waist. John preached a message of repentance for the forgiveness of sins, and foretold the coming of Jesus as the Messiah. Many people from all over Judea came to listen to John's message and be baptized by him in the River Jordan.

Baptism of Christ

Pieter de Campana

c. 1540

Jesus was baptized in the River Jordan by John the Baptist, seen here on the right of the painting leaning down to scoop up a bowl of water. The Holy Spirit in the form of a dove can be seen descending from the heavens.

In those days, Jesus came from Nazareth of Galilee, and was baptized by John in the Jordan. Immediately coming up from the water, he saw the heavens parting, and the Spirit descending on him like a dove. A voice came out of the sky, "You are my beloved Son, in whom I am well pleased."

Mark 1:9–11

The beginning of the Good News of Jesus Christ, the Son of God. ² As it is written in the prophets:
"Behold, I send my messenger
   before your face,
who will prepare your way before you:
³   the voice of one crying in the wilderness,
   'Make ready the way of the Lord!
      Make his paths straight!'"
⁴ John came baptizing in the wilderness and preaching the baptism of repentance for forgiveness of sins. ⁵ All the country of Judea and all those of Jerusalem went out to him. They were baptized by him in the Jordan river, confessing their sins. ⁶ John was clothed with camel's hair and a leather belt around his waist. He ate locusts and wild honey. ⁷ He preached, saying, "After me comes he who is mightier than I, the thong of whose sandals I am not worthy to stoop down and loosen.

⁸ I baptized you with water, but he will baptize you with the Holy Spirit."

⁹ In those days, Jesus came from Nazareth of Galilee, and was baptized by John in the Jordan. ¹⁰ Immediately coming up from the water, he saw the heavens parting, and the Spirit descending on him like a dove. ¹¹ A voice came out of the sky, "You are my beloved Son, in whom I am well pleased."

¹² Immediately the Spirit drove him out into the wilderness. ¹³ He was there in the wilderness forty days tempted by Satan. He was with the wild animals; and the angels were serving him.

¹⁴ Now after John was taken into custody, Jesus came into Galilee, preaching the Good News of God's Kingdom, ¹⁵ and saying, "The time is fulfilled, and God's Kingdom is at hand! Repent, and believe in the Good News."

Christ's Temptation

Dutch School

C. 16TH CENTURY

After being baptized, Jesus spent forty days in the wilderness, where he was tempted by Satan and ministered by angels. Mark's Gospel describes this event briefly, but the Gospels of Matthew and Luke give details of Satan's temptations. Here, a bestial Satan offers a stone to Jesus, saying that if Jesus is the Son of God, then he should turn the stone to bread. Jesus refused, saying that man shall not live by bread alone, but by the word of God.

Immediately the Spirit drove him out into the wilderness. He was there in the wilderness forty days tempted by Satan. He was with the wild animals; and the angels were serving him.

Mark 1:12–13

16 Passing along by the sea of Galilee, he saw Simon and Andrew the brother of Simon casting a net into the sea, for they were fishermen. 17 Jesus said to them, "Come after me, and I will make you into fishers for men."

18 Immediately they left their nets, and followed him. 19 Going on a little further from there, he saw James the son of Zebedee, and John, his brother, who were also in the boat mending the nets. 20 Immediately he called them, and they left their father, Zebedee, in the boat with the hired servants, and went after him. 21 They went into Capernaum, and immediately on the Sabbath day he entered into the synagogue and taught. 22 They were astonished at his teaching, for he taught them as having authority, and not as the scribes. 23 Immediately there was in their synagogue a man with an unclean spirit, and he cried out, 24 saying, "Ha! What do we have to do with

you, Jesus, you Nazarene? Have you come to destroy us? I know you who you are: the Holy One of God!"

25 Jesus rebuked him, saying, "Be quiet, and come out of him!"

26 The unclean spirit, convulsing him and crying with a loud voice, came out of him. 27 They were all amazed, so that they questioned among themselves, saying, "What is this? A new teaching? For with authority he commands even the unclean spirits, and they obey him!" 28 The report of him went out immediately everywhere into all the region of Galilee and its surrounding area.

29 Immediately, when they had come out of the synagogue, they came into the house of Simon and Andrew, with James and John. 30 Now Simon's wife's mother lay sick with a fever, and immediately they told him about her. 31 He came and took her by the hand, and raised her up. The fever left her, and

Vocation of the Apostles

Domenico Ghirlandaio
1481–82

This fresco, located in the Sistine Chapel in Rome, Italy, depicts the story of the first four disciples to be called by Jesus to follow him. Peter (wearing a yellow/orange cloak) and Andrew (green cloak) kneel before Jesus as he blesses them in the foreground of the painting. Other parts of the story can be seen in the background, where the figure of Jesus is shown calling to Peter and Andrew in their fishing boat on the left, and then later to James and John in a fishing boat on the right, with Peter and Andrew standing behind Jesus on the shore.

she served them. **32** At evening, when the sun had set, they brought to him all who were sick, and those who were possessed by demons. **33** All the city was gathered together at the door. **34** He healed many who were sick with various diseases, and cast out many demons. He did not allow the demons to speak, because they knew him.

35 Early in the morning, while it was still dark, he rose up and went out, and departed into a deserted place, and prayed there. **36** Simon and those who were with him followed after him; **37** and they found him, and told him, "Everyone is looking for you."

38 He said to them, "Let's go elsewhere into the next towns, that I may preach there also, because I came out for this reason." **39** He went into their synagogues throughout all Galilee, preaching and casting out demons.

40 A leper came to him, begging him, kneeling down to him, and saying to him, "If you want to, you can make me clean."

41 Being moved with compassion, he stretched out his hand, and touched him, and said to him, "I want to. Be made clean." **42** When he had said this, immediately the leprosy departed from him, and he was made clean. **43** He strictly warned him, and immediately sent him out, **44** and said to him, "See you say nothing to anybody, but go show yourself to the priest, and offer for your cleansing the things which Moses commanded, for a testimony to them."

45 But he went out, and began to proclaim it much, and to spread about the matter, so that Jesus could no more openly enter into a city, but was outside in desert places: and they came to him from everywhere.

Jesus in Capernaum

Rodolfo Amoedo
1885
Jesus began his public ministry in Capernaum, and it was the location of numerous miracles and parables. This oil study shows Jesus walking through the streets of Capernaum, followed by a crowd of people wanting to hear him preach, while others bring sick people to be healed.

CHAPTER 2

Jesus heals a paralyzed man by telling the man that his sins are forgiven. The scribes question Jesus' authority to forgive sins. When Jesus is seen eating and drinking with sinners and tax collectors, the scribes and Pharisees ask why he does so. Jesus replies that he has come to call sinners to repentance, not the righteous. More controversies follow about why Jesus' disciples do not fast and why they pick grain on the Sabbath day when it is not lawful to do so.

His disciples began . . . to pluck the ears of grain. Mark 2:23

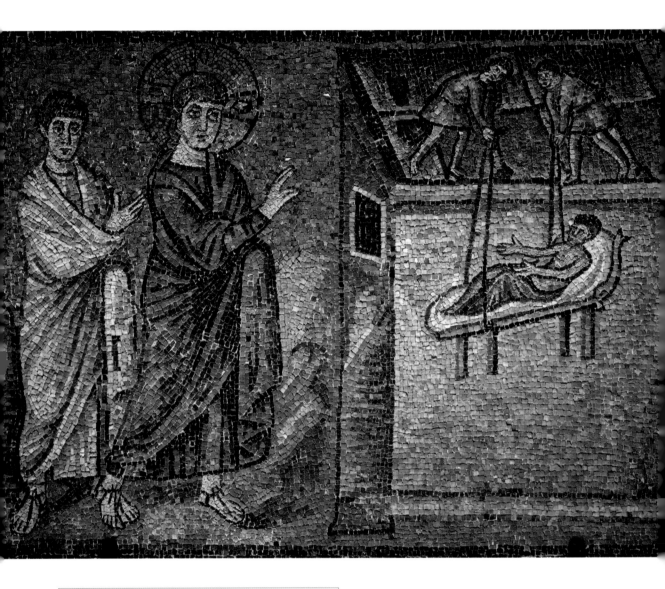

The Healing of the Paralytic at Capernaum

Italian School

EARLY 6TH CENTURY

This Byzantine mosaic in the Basilica of Sant'Apollinare Nuovo in Ravenna, Italy, is one of thirteen panels depicting the miracles and parables of Jesus. This one shows the story of the paralyzed man being lowered down through the roof of a house because the doorway was too crowded to gain entry. Jesus, in Roman dress with a cruciform halo, can be seen giving the sign of benediction, forgiving the man his sins and restoring his ability to walk.

Four people came, carrying a paralytic to him. When they could not come near to him for the crowd, they removed the roof where he was. When they had broken it up, they let down the mat that the paralytic was lying on. Jesus, seeing their faith, said to the paralytic, "Son, your sins are forgiven you."

Mark 2:3–5

When he entered again into Capernaum after some days, it was heard that he was in the house. **2** Immediately many were gathered together, so that there was no more room, not even around the door; and he spoke the word to them. **3** Four people came, carrying a paralytic to him. **4** When they could not come near to him for the crowd, they removed the roof where he was. When they had broken it up, they let down the mat that the paralytic was lying on. **5** Jesus, seeing their faith, said to the paralytic, "Son, your sins are forgiven you."

6 But there were some of the scribes sitting there, and reasoning in their hearts, **7** "Why does this man speak blasphemies like that? Who can forgive sins but God alone?"

8 Immediately Jesus, perceiving in his spirit that they so reasoned within themselves, said to them, "Why do you reason these things in your hearts? **9** Which is easier, to tell the paralytic, 'Your sins are forgiven'; or to say, 'Arise, and take up your bed, and walk?' **10** But that you may know that the Son of Man has authority on earth to forgive sins"—he said to the paralytic— **11** "I tell you, arise, take up your mat, and go to your house."

12 He arose, and immediately took up the mat, and went out in front of them all; so that they were all amazed, and glorified God, saying, "We never saw anything like this!"

13 He went out again by the seaside. All the multitude came to him, and he taught them. **14** As he passed by, he saw Levi [*also called Matthew*], the son of Alphaeus, sitting at the tax office, and he said to him, "Follow me." And he arose and followed him.

15 He was reclining at the table in his house, and many tax collectors and sinners sat down with Jesus and his disciples, for there were many, and they followed him. **16** The scribes and the Pharisees, when they saw that he was eating with the sinners and tax collectors, said to his disciples, "Why is it that he eats and drinks with tax collectors and sinners?"

17 When Jesus heard it, he said to them, "Those who are healthy have no need for a physician, but those who are sick. I came not to call the righteous, but sinners to repentance."

18 John's disciples and the Pharisees were fasting, and they came and asked him, "Why do John's disciples and the disciples of the Pharisees fast, but your disciples don't fast?"

19 Jesus said to them, "Can the groomsmen fast while the bridegroom is with them? As long as they have the bridegroom with them, they can't fast. **20** But the days will come when

The Feast in the House of Levi

Paolo Veronese
1573

This painting is a section of a large—18 x 42-foot (5.5 x 12.8-meter)—canvas that was created for the refectory wall of a Dominican friary in Italy. Originally depicting the Last Supper, Church authorities were upset at the inclusion of indecorous figures such as "drunken buffoons, armed Germans, dwarfs, and similar scurrilities" and ordered the artist to change the painting. Instead, Veronese retitled it to depict the story of Jesus eating with tax collectors and sinners in the home of the disciple Levi (also called Matthew).

the bridegroom will be taken away from them, and then will they fast in that day. **21** No one sews a piece of unshrunk cloth on an old garment, or else the patch shrinks and the new tears away from the old, and a worse hole is made. **22** No one puts new wine into old wineskins, or else the new wine will burst the skins, and the wine pours out, and the skins will be destroyed; but they put new wine into fresh wineskins."

23 He was going on the Sabbath day through the grain fields, and his disciples began, as they went, to pluck the ears of grain. **24** The Pharisees said to him, "Behold, why do they do that which is not lawful on the Sabbath day?"

25 He said to them, "Did you never read what David did, when he had need, and was hungry—he, and those who were with him? **26** How he entered into God's house when Abiathar was high priest, and ate the consecrated bread, which is not lawful to eat except for the priests, and gave also to those who were with him?" **27** He said to them, "The Sabbath was made for man, not man for the Sabbath. **28** Therefore the Son of Man is lord even of the Sabbath."

Christ and the Disciples, or Breaking the Law

Károly Markó the Younger
1854

Jesus and his disciples are seen walking by a ripe grainfield in an idyllic landscape, with some of the disciples eating freshly picked grain. Several Pharisees are questioning Jesus about why the disciples are breaking the law by harvesting—that is, working— on the Sabbath day. This is one of several occasions when Jesus clashed with religious leaders over the interpretation and observance of Sabbath laws.

CHAPTER 3

Jesus heals a man with a withered hand on the Sabbath day. The Pharisees then conspire with the Herodians about how they might destroy Jesus. As news of Jesus' deeds spread, more and more people begin to follow him. Jesus appoints twelve disciples— also called the twelve apostles—to be with him and to be sent out to preach, heal, and cast out demons. Jesus refutes the scribes' claim that he casts out demons with the help of Satan. Jesus says that all the sins of man will be forgiven except for blasphemy against the Holy Spirit.

The unclean spirits...fell down before him. Mark 3:11

He appointed twelve, that they might be with him, and that he might send them out to preach, and to have authority to heal sicknesses and to cast out demons.

Mark 3:14–15

He entered again into the synagogue, and there was a man there who had his hand withered. 2 They watched him, whether he would heal him on the Sabbath day, that they might accuse him. 3 He said to the man who had his hand withered, "Stand up." 4 He said to them, "Is it lawful on the Sabbath day to do good, or to do harm? To save a life, or to kill?" But they were silent. 5 When he had looked around at them with anger, being grieved at the hardening of their hearts, he said to the man, "Stretch out your hand." He stretched it out, and his hand was restored as healthy as the other. 6 The Pharisees went out, and immediately conspired with the Herodians against him, how they might destroy him.

7 Jesus withdrew to the sea with his disciples, and a great multitude followed him from Galilee, from Judea, 8 from Jerusalem, from Idumaea, beyond the Jordan, and those from around Tyre and Sidon. A great multitude, hearing what great things he did, came to him. 9 He spoke to his disciples that a little boat should stay near him because of the crowd, so that they wouldn't press on him. 10 For he had healed many, so that as many as had diseases pressed on him that they might touch him. 11 The unclean spirits, whenever they saw him, fell down before him, and cried, "You are the Son of God!" 12 He sternly warned them that they should not make him known.

13 He went up into the mountain, and called to himself those whom he wanted, and they went to him. 14 He appointed twelve, that they might be with him, and that he might send them out to preach, 15 and to have authority to heal sicknesses and to cast out demons: 16 Simon, to whom he gave the name Peter; 17 James the son of Zebedee; John, the brother of James, and he called them Boanerges, which means, Sons of Thunder; 18 Andrew; Philip; Bartholomew; Matthew; Thomas; James, the son of Alphaeus; Thaddaeus; Simon the Zealot; 19 and Judas Iscariot, who also betrayed him.

He came into a house. 20 The multitude came together again, so that they could not so much as eat bread. 21 When his friends heard it, they went out to seize him: for they said,

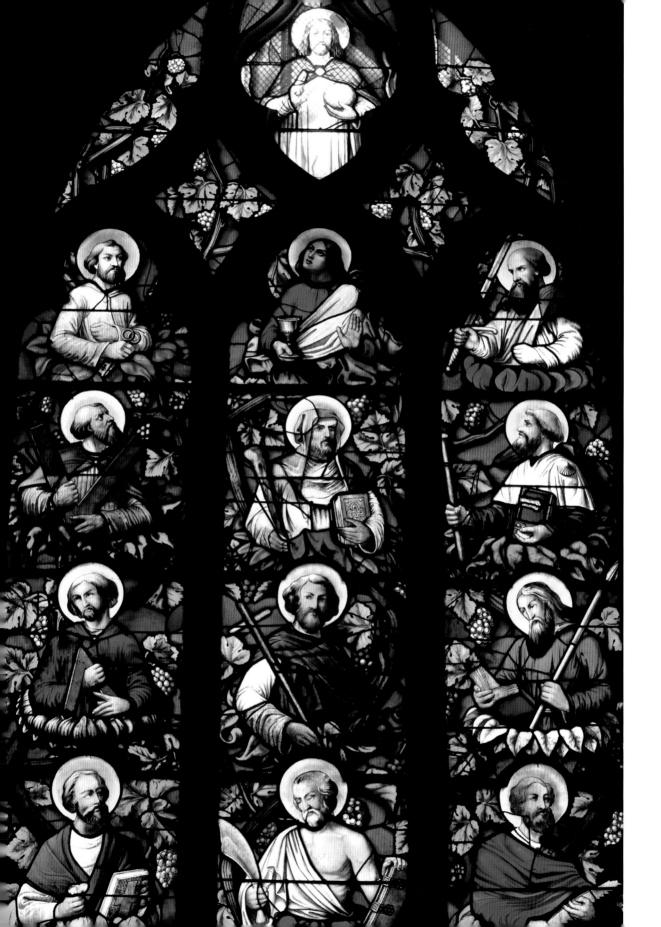

"He is insane." **22** The scribes who came down from Jerusalem said, "He has Beelzebul," and, "By the prince of the demons he casts out the demons."

23 He summoned them, and said to them in parables, "How can Satan cast out Satan? **24** If a kingdom is divided against itself, that kingdom cannot stand. **25** If a house is divided against itself, that house cannot stand. **26** If Satan has risen up against himself, and is divided, he can't stand, but has an end. **27** But no one can enter into the house of the strong man to plunder, unless he first binds the strong man; and then he will plunder his house. **28** Most certainly I tell you, all sins of the descendants of man will be forgiven, including their blasphemies with which they may blaspheme; **29** but whoever may blaspheme against the Holy Spirit never has forgiveness, but is subject to eternal condemnation." **30** —he said this because they had said, "He has an unclean spirit."

31 His mother and his brothers came, and standing outside, they sent to him, calling him. **32** A multitude was sitting around him, and they told him, "Behold, your mother, your brothers, and your sisters are outside looking for you."

33 He answered them, "Who are my mother and my brothers?" **34** Looking around at those who sat around him, he said, "Behold, my mother and my brothers! **35** For whoever does the will of God, the same is my brother, and my sister, and mother."

The Pharisees and the Herodians Conspire Against Jesus

James Tissot
1886–94

This painting from *The Life of Our Lord Jesus Christ*, a series of 350 watercolors illustrating the Gospels, shows a group of Pharisees and Herodians plotting against Jesus. During the New Testament era, when Judea was a province of the Roman Empire, there were several significant political and religious groups. The Pharisees, who were strict and legalistic, controlled the synagogues. The Herodians were supporters of the ruling Herodian dynasty of puppet kings installed by Rome.

CHAPTER 4

Jesus sits in a boat as crowds gather around the shore and begins to teach them through the use of parables. Jesus reflects on how a farmer's seed will only yield fruit when sown on good soil. Seed sown by the road, on rocky ground, or among thorns will not prosper. Similarly, Jesus' own message will not be understood or accepted by everyone. In private, Jesus explains all of his parables to the disciples. When the disciples are caught in the boat during a storm, Jesus calms the storm.

Again he began to teach by the seaside. Mark 4:1

The Parable of the Sower

Jacopo Bassano

c. 1560

The artist treats this religious subject as a genre painting—the depiction of an everyday scene with ordinary people going about their daily lives. The sower from the parable is in the field behind the women and children, who are preparing a meal and tending to the animals.

"Those which were sown on the good ground are those who hear the word, and accept it, and bear fruit, some thirty times, some sixty times, and some one hundred times."

Mark 4:20

Again he began to teach by the seaside. A great multitude was gathered to him, so that he entered into a boat in the sea, and sat down. All the multitude were on the land by the sea. 2 He taught them many things in parables, and told them in his teaching, 3 "Listen! Behold, the farmer went out to sow, 4 and as he sowed, some seed fell by the road, and the birds came and devoured it. 5 Others fell on the rocky ground, where it had little soil, and immediately it sprang up, because it had no depth of soil. 6 When the sun had risen, it was scorched; and because it had no root, it withered away. 7 Others fell among the thorns, and the thorns grew up, and choked it, and it yielded no fruit. 8 Others fell into the good ground, and yielded fruit, growing up and increasing. Some produced thirty times, some sixty times, and some one hundred times as much." 9 He said, "Whoever has ears to hear, let him hear."

10 When he was alone, those who were around him with the twelve asked him about the parables. 11 He said to them, "To you is given the mystery of God's Kingdom, but to those who are outside, all things are done in parables, 12 that 'seeing they may see, and not perceive; and hearing they may hear, and not understand; lest perhaps they should turn again, and their sins should be forgiven them.'"

13 He said to them, "Don't you understand this parable? How will you understand all of the parables? 14 The farmer sows the word. 15 The ones by the road are the ones where the word is sown; and when they have heard, immediately Satan comes, and takes away the word which has been sown in them. 16 These in the same way are those who are sown on the rocky places, who, when they have heard the word, immediately receive it with joy. 17 They have no root in themselves, but are short-lived. When oppression or persecution arises because of the word, immediately they stumble. 18 Others are those who are sown among the thorns. These are those who have heard the word, 19 and the cares of this age, and the deceitfulness of riches, and the lusts of other things entering in choke the word, and it becomes unfruitful. 20 Those which were sown on the good ground are those who hear the word, and accept it, and bear fruit, some thirty times, some sixty times, and some one hundred times."

**Christ in the Storm
on the Sea of Galilee**

Rembrandt van Rijn

1633

This dramatic painting is Rembrandt's only known seascape. It shows the terrified disciples, caught in a great storm and struggling to control the boat, as they wake a sleeping Jesus (second from right, in purple cloak). Jesus miraculously calmed the storm, striking awe into the disciples.

He awoke, and rebuked the wind, and said to the sea, "Peace! Be still!" The wind ceased, and there was a great calm.

Mark 4:39

²¹ He said to them, "Is the lamp brought to be put under a basket or under a bed? Isn't it put on a stand? ²² For there is nothing hidden, except that it should be made known; neither was anything made secret, but that it should come to light. ²³ If any man has ears to hear, let him hear."

²⁴ He said to them, "Take heed what you hear. With whatever measure you measure, it will be measured to you, and more will be given to you who hear. ²⁵ For whoever has, to him will more be given, and he who doesn't have, even that which he has will be taken away from him."

²⁶ He said, "God's Kingdom is as if a man should cast seed on the earth, ²⁷ and should sleep and rise night and day, and the seed should spring up and grow, he doesn't know how. ²⁸ For the earth bears fruit: first the blade, then the ear, then the full grain in the ear. ²⁹ But when the fruit is ripe, immediately he puts in the sickle, because the harvest has come."

³⁰ He said, "How will we liken God's Kingdom? Or with what parable will we illustrate it? ³¹ It's like a grain of mustard seed, which, when it is sown in the earth, though it is less than all the seeds that are on the earth, ³² yet when it is sown, grows up, and becomes greater than all the herbs, and puts out great branches, so that the birds of the sky can lodge under its shadow."

³³ With many such parables he spoke the word to them, as they were able to hear it. ³⁴ Without a parable he didn't speak to them; but privately to his own disciples he explained everything.

³⁵ On that day, when evening had come, he said to them, "Let's go over to the other side." ³⁶ Leaving the multitude, they took him with them, even as he was, in the boat. Other small boats were also with him. ³⁷ A big wind storm arose, and the waves beat into the boat, so much that the boat was already filled. ³⁸ He himself was in the stern, asleep on the cushion, and they woke him up, and told him, "Teacher, don't you care that we are dying?"

³⁹ He awoke, and rebuked the wind, and said to the sea, "Peace! Be still!" The wind ceased, and there was a great calm. ⁴⁰ He said to them, "Why are you so afraid? How is it that you have no faith?"

⁴¹ They were greatly afraid, and said to one another, "Who then is this, that even the wind and the sea obey him?"

CHAPTER 5

Jesus encounters a man possessed by many demons whom nobody can subdue. Jesus orders the demons to leave, but they beg to be allowed to enter a herd of pigs nearby. Jesus agrees, but when they do so, the herd rushes into the sea and drowns. A woman with a hemorrhage touches Jesus' clothes and is cured because of her faith. Jairus, the ruler of a synagogue, asks Jesus to heal his daughter. When told that the girl has just died, Jesus says that she is merely sleeping. He tells her to rise and she does so.

Nobody had the strength to tame him. Mark 5:4

They came to the other side of the sea, into the country of the Gadarenes. ² When he had come out of the boat, immediately a man with an unclean spirit met him out of the tombs. ³ He lived in the tombs. Nobody could bind him any more, not even with chains, ⁴ because he had been often bound with fetters and chains, and the chains had been torn apart by him, and the fetters broken in pieces. Nobody had the strength to tame him. ⁵ Always, night and day, in the tombs and in the mountains, he was crying out, and cutting himself with stones. ⁶ When he saw Jesus from afar, he ran and bowed down to him, ⁷ and crying out with a loud voice, he said, "What have I to do with you, Jesus, you Son of the Most High God? I adjure you by God, don't torment me." ⁸ For he said to him, "Come out of the man, you unclean spirit!"

⁹ He asked him, "What is your name?"

He said to him, "My name is Legion, for we are many." ¹⁰ He begged him much that he would not send them away out of the country. ¹¹ Now on the mountainside there was a great herd of pigs feeding. ¹² All the demons begged him, saying, "Send us into the pigs, that we may enter into them."

¹³ At once Jesus gave them permission. The unclean spirits came out and entered into the pigs. The herd of about two thousand rushed down the steep bank into the sea, and they were drowned in the sea. ¹⁴ Those who fed them fled, and told it in the city and in the country.

The people came to see what it was that had happened. ¹⁵ They came to Jesus, and saw him who had been possessed by demons sitting, clothed, and in his right mind, even him who had the legion; and they were afraid. ¹⁶ Those who saw it declared to them what happened to him who was possessed by demons, and about the pigs. ¹⁷ They began to beg him to depart from their region.

¹⁸ As he was entering into the boat, he who had been possessed by demons begged him that he might be with him. ¹⁹ He did not allow him, but said to him, "Go to your house, to your friends, and tell them what great things the Lord has done for you, and how he had mercy on you."

²⁰ He went his way, and began to proclaim in Decapolis how Jesus had done great things for him, and everyone marveled.

²¹ When Jesus had crossed back over in the boat to the other side, a great multitude was gathered to him; and he was by the sea. ²² Behold, one of the rulers of the synagogue, Jairus by name, came; and seeing him, he fell at his feet, ²³ and begged him much, saying, "My little daughter is at the point of death. Please come and lay your hands on her, that she may be made healthy, and live."

²⁴ He went with him, and a great multitude followed him, and they pressed upon him on all sides. ²⁵ A certain woman, who had been bleeding for twelve years, ²⁶ and had suffered many things by many physicians, and had spent all that she had, and was no better, but rather grew worse, ²⁷ having heard the things concerning Jesus, came up behind him in the crowd, and touched his clothes. ²⁸ For she said, "If I just touch his clothes, I will be made well." ²⁹ Immediately the flow of her blood was dried up, and she felt in her body that she was healed of her affliction.

³⁰ Immediately Jesus, perceiving in himself that the power had gone out from him, turned around in the crowd, and asked, "Who touched my clothes?"

³¹ His disciples said to him, "You see the multitude pressing against you, and you say, 'Who touched me?'"

³² He looked around to see her who had done this thing. ³³ But the woman, fearing and trembling, knowing what had been done to her, came and fell down before him, and told him all the truth.

³⁴ He said to her, "Daughter, your faith has made you well. Go in peace, and be cured of your disease."

The Healing of the Woman Diseased with an Issue of Blood

Italian School

12th–13TH CENTURY

The interior of the Cathedral of Monreale in Italy is covered with exquisite mosaics depicting religious figures and stories. Here, a woman who has suffered from a hemorrhage (an issue of blood) for twelve years touches Jesus' cloak and is healed because of her faith.

35 While he was still speaking, people came from the synagogue ruler's house saying, "Your daughter is dead. Why bother the Teacher any more?"

36 But Jesus, when he heard the message spoken, immediately said to the ruler of the synagogue, "Don't be afraid, only believe." **37** He allowed no one to follow him, except Peter, James, and John the brother of James. **38** He came to the synagogue ruler's house, and he saw an uproar, weeping, and great wailing. **39** When he had entered in, he said to them, "Why do you make an uproar and weep? The child is not dead, but is asleep."

40 They ridiculed him. But he, having put them all out, took the father of the child, her mother, and those who were with him, and went in where the child was lying. **41** Taking the child by the hand, he said to her, "Talitha cumi!" which means, being interpreted, "Girl, I tell you, get up!" **42** Immediately the girl rose up and walked, for she was twelve years old. They were greatly amazed. **43** He strictly ordered them that no one should know this, and commanded that something should be given to her to eat.

The Raising of Jairus's Daughter

Johann Friedrich Overbeck

c. 1809

Jairus, one of the rulers of a synagogue, asked Jesus to come to his home and heal his sick daughter. Despite being told on the way that the girl had died, Jesus continued to the house. In this painting Jesus is holding the girl's hand and telling her to rise. The girl's parents are on the left, and the disciples Peter, James, and John are on the right.

CHAPTER 6

Jesus is rejected at Nazareth, the place where he grew up. He sends out the twelve disciples on their first mission to preach and heal. King Herod hears of Jesus and thinks he is John the Baptist—whom Herod had beheaded at the request of his step-daughter, Salome—risen from the dead. After preaching to a multitude of five thousand people, Jesus miraculously feeds everyone with only five loaves and two fish. When the disciples are out rowing in a boat in adverse winds, Jesus walks across the water to them and calms the wind.

"Give me…the head of John the Baptist on a platter." Mark 6:25

He went out from there. He came into his own country, and his disciples followed him. **2** When the Sabbath had come, he began to teach in the synagogue, and many hearing him were astonished, saying, "Where did this man get these things?" and, "What is the wisdom that is given to this man, that such mighty works come about by his hands? **3** Isn't this the carpenter, the son of Mary, and brother of James, Joses, Judah, and Simon? Aren't his sisters here with us?" They were offended at him.

4 Jesus said to them, "A prophet is not without honor, except in his own country, and among his own relatives, and in his own house." **5** He could do no mighty work there, except that he laid his hands on a few sick people, and healed them. **6** He marveled because of their unbelief.

He went around the villages teaching. **7** He called to himself the twelve, and began to send them out two by two; and he gave them authority over the unclean spirits. **8** He commanded them that they should take nothing for their journey, except a staff only: no bread, no wallet, no money in their purse, **9** but to wear sandals, and not put on two tunics. **10** He said to them, "Wherever you enter into a house, stay there until you depart from there. **11** Whoever will not receive you

nor hear you, as you depart from there, shake off the dust that is under your feet for a testimony against them. Assuredly, I tell you, it will be more tolerable for Sodom and Gomorrah in the day of judgment than for that city!"

12 They went out and preached that people should repent. **13** They cast out many demons, and anointed many with oil who were sick, and healed them. **14** King Herod heard this, for his name had become known, and he said, "John the Baptist has risen from the dead, and therefore these powers are at work in him." **15** But others said, "He is Elijah." Others said, "He is a prophet, or like one of the prophets." **16** But Herod, when he heard this, said, "This is John, whom I beheaded. He has risen from the dead." **17** For Herod himself had sent out and arrested John, and bound him in prison for the sake of Herodias, his brother Philip's wife, for he had married her. **18** For John said to Herod, "It is not lawful for you to have your brother's wife." **19** Herodias set herself against him, and desired to kill him, but she could not, **20** for Herod feared John, knowing that he was a righteous and holy man, and kept him safe. When he heard him, he did many things, and he heard him gladly.

21 Then a convenient day came, that Herod on his birthday made a supper for his nobles, the high officers, and the chief men of Galilee. **22** When the daughter of Herodias herself came in and danced, she pleased Herod and those sitting with him. The king said to the young lady, "Ask me whatever you want, and I will give it to you." **23** He swore to her, "Whatever you shall ask of me, I will give you, up to half of my kingdom."

24 She went out, and said to her mother, "What shall I ask?"

She said, "The head of John the Baptist."

25 She came in immediately with haste to the king, and asked, "I want you to give me right now the head of John the Baptist on a platter."

26 The king was exceedingly sorry, but for the sake of his oaths, and of his dinner guests, he did not wish to refuse her. **27** Immediately the king sent out a soldier of his guard, and commanded to bring John's head, and he went and beheaded him in the prison, **28** and brought his head on a platter, and gave it to the young lady; and the young lady gave it to her mother. **29** When his disciples heard

Salome Receives the Head of John the Baptist

Michelangelo Merisi da Caravaggio
1607–1610

Here, Salome looks away from the head of John the Baptist. She danced so well for her step-father King Herod that he granted her any request. At the urging of her mother, Herodias, who sought vengeance against John the Baptist for disapproving of her marriage, Salome requested John's head.

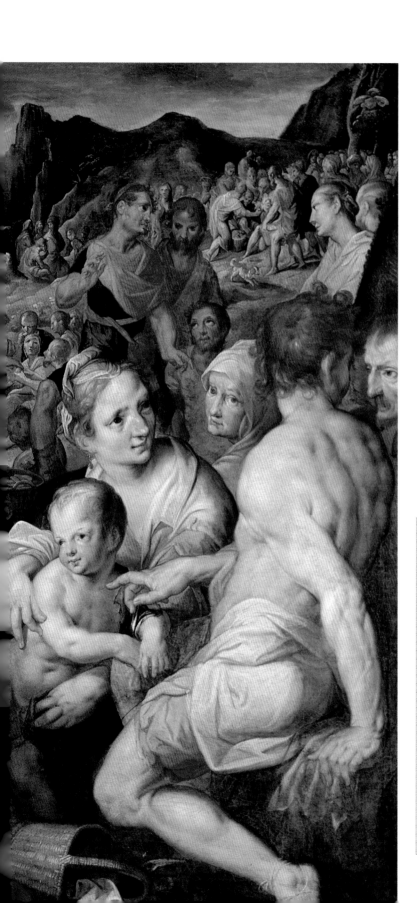

The Feeding of the Five Thousand

Ambrosius Francken the Elder

16th–17TH CENTURY

A multitude of five thousand people gathered to hear Jesus preach. When the day grew late, the disciples asked Jesus whether they should send everyone away so that they could buy something to eat. Jesus told the disciples to gather what food they had—only five loaves of bread and two fish. This painting shows the moment when Jesus looks up to heaven and blesses the food, which is then miraculously divided among the multitude of people, all of whom eat until satisfied.

this, they came and took up his corpse, and laid it in a tomb.

30 The apostles gathered themselves together to Jesus, and they told him all things, whatever they had done, and whatever they had taught. **31** He said to them, "You come apart into a deserted place, and rest awhile." For there were many coming and going, and they had no leisure so much as to eat. **32** They went away in the boat to a deserted place by themselves. **33** They saw them going, and many recognized him and ran there on foot from all the cities. They arrived before them and came together to him. **34** Jesus came out, saw a great multitude, and he had compassion on them, because they were like sheep without a shepherd, and he began to teach them many things. **35** When it was late in the day, his disciples came to him, and said, "This place is deserted, and it is late in the day. **36** Send them away, that they may go into the surrounding country and villages, and buy themselves bread, for they have nothing to eat."

37 But he answered them, "You give them something to eat."

They asked him, "Shall we go and buy two hundred denarii worth of bread [*200 denarii was about seven or eight months' wages for an agricultural laborer*], and give them something to eat?"

38 He said to them, "How many loaves do you have? Go see."

When they knew, they said, "Five, and two fish."

39 He commanded them that everyone should sit down in groups on the green grass. **40** They sat down in ranks, by hundreds and by fifties. **41** He took the five loaves and the two fish, and looking up to heaven, he blessed and broke the loaves, and he gave to his disciples to set before them, and he divided the two fish among them all. **42** They all ate, and were filled. **43** They took up twelve baskets full of broken pieces and also of the fish. **44** Those who ate the loaves were five thousand men.

45 Immediately he made his disciples get into the boat, and to go ahead to the other side, to Bethsaida, while he himself sent the multitude away. **46** After he had taken leave of them, he went up the mountain to pray.

47 When evening had come, the boat was in the middle of the sea, and he was alone on the land. **48** Seeing them distressed in rowing, for the wind was contrary to them, about the fourth watch of the night he came to them, walking on the sea, and he would have passed by them, **49** but they, when they saw him walking on the sea, supposed that it was a ghost, and cried out; **50** for they all saw him, and were troubled. But he immediately spoke with them, and said to them, "Take heart, it is I! Don't be afraid." **51** He got into the boat with them; and the wind ceased, and they were very amazed among themselves, and marveled; **52** for they had not understood about the loaves, but their hearts were hardened.

53 When they had crossed over, they came to land at Gennesaret, and moored to the shore. **54** When they had come out of the boat, immediately the people recognized him, **55** and ran around that whole region, and began to bring those who were sick, on their mats, to where they heard he was. **56** Wherever he entered, into villages, or into cities, or into the country, they laid the sick in the marketplaces, and begged him that they might touch just the fringe of his garment; and as many as touched him were made well.

Jesus Walking Upon the Sea

William Hole

c. 1906

This watercolor is one of 80 illustrations that appeared in *The Life of Jesus of Nazareth*, first published in 1906. Jesus is seen walking over the water to the boat where the disciples are struggling to row against adverse winds. At first the disciples feared that the figure coming toward them was a ghost—an impression emphasized in the painting by the dramatic moonlight and white clothing of Jesus.

CHAPTER 7

The Pharisees and scribes ask Jesus why some of his disciples eat with unwashed hands, rather than wash in accordance with the traditions of the elders. Jesus calls them hypocrites for holding to man's traditions but setting aside God's commandments. He tells everyone that man can only be defiled by the sins coming from within him, not by the foods he puts into his body. Jesus travels farther afield and cures a Gentile woman's daughter. Back in Galilee, he restores a man's hearing and speech.

She begged him [to] cast the demon out of her daughter. Mark 7:26

Then the Pharisees and some of the scribes gathered together to him, having come from Jerusalem. ² Now when they saw some of his disciples eating bread with defiled, that is unwashed, hands, they found fault. ³ (For the Pharisees, and all the Jews, don't eat unless they wash their hands and forearms, holding to the tradition of the elders. ⁴ They don't eat when they come from the marketplace unless they bathe themselves, and there are many other traditions that they observe: washings of cups, pitchers, bronze vessels, and couches.) ⁵ The Pharisees and the scribes asked him, "Why don't your disciples walk according to the tradition of the elders, but eat their bread with unwashed hands?"

⁶ He answered them, "Well did Isaiah prophesy of you hypocrites, as it is written:
    'This people honors me with their lips,
        but their heart is far from me.
⁷   But they worship me in vain,
        teaching as doctrines the
        commandments of men.'

⁸ "For you set aside the commandment of God, and hold tightly to the tradition of men—the washing of pitchers and cups, and you do many other such things." ⁹ He said to them, "Full well do you reject the commandment of God, that you may keep your tradition. ¹⁰ For Moses said, 'Honor your father and your mother'; and, 'He who speaks evil of father or mother, let him be put to death.' ¹¹ But you say, 'If a man tells his father or his mother, "Whatever profit you might have received from me is Corban, that is to

Christ Disputing with the Pharisees

Jacob Jordaens
17TH CENTURY

Jesus and the Pharisees disputed with each other about why Jesus and his disciples did not observe all of the laws and traditions of the elders. Here, Jesus is shown at the center of the painting with the Holy Spirit above him in the form of a dove, while on either side of him the Pharisees consult their documents.

The Woman Begging Jesus to Heal Her Possessed Daughter

Cristoforo de Predis
1476

This image is from the *Predis Codex*, a bound collection of the artist's miniature paintings of biblical scenes. It depicts the story of a Gentile woman whom Jesus met when traveling between Tyre and Sidon. Here, she is seen approaching Jesus and begging him to heal her possessed daughter.

For a woman, whose little daughter had an unclean spirit, having heard of him, came and fell down at his feet. Now the woman was a Greek, a Syrophoenician by race. She begged him that he would cast the demon out of her daughter.

Mark 7:25–26

say, given to God" '; **12** then you no longer allow him to do anything for his father or his mother, **13** making void the word of God by your tradition, which you have handed down. You do many things like this."

14 He called all the multitude to himself, and said to them, "Hear me, all of you, and understand. **15** There is nothing from outside of the man, that going into him can defile him; but the things which proceed out of the man are those that defile the man. **16** If anyone has ears to hear, let him hear!"

17 When he had entered into a house away from the multitude, his disciples asked him about the parable. **18** He said to them, "Are you also without understanding? Don't you perceive that whatever goes into the man from outside can't defile him, **19** because it doesn't go into his heart, but into his stomach, then into the latrine?" (Thus he declared all foods clean.) **20** He said, "That which proceeds out of the man, that defiles the man. **21** For from within, out of the hearts of men, proceed evil thoughts, adulteries, sexual sins, murders, thefts, **22** covetings, wickedness, deceit, lustful desires, an evil eye, blasphemy, pride, and foolishness. **23** All these evil things come from within, and defile the man."

24 From there he arose, and went away into the borders of Tyre and Sidon. He entered into a house, and did not want anyone to know it, but he could not escape notice. **25** For a woman, whose little daughter had an unclean spirit, having heard of him, came and fell down at his feet. **26** Now the woman was a Greek, a Syrophoenician by race. She begged him that he would cast the demon out of her daughter. **27** But Jesus said to her, "First let the children eat their fill, for it is not appropriate to take the children's bread and throw it to the dogs."

28 But she answered him, "Yes, Lord. Yet even the dogs under the table eat the children's crumbs."

29 He said to her, "For this saying, go your way. The demon has gone out of your daughter."

30 She went away to her house, and found the child having been laid on the bed, with the demon gone out.

31 Again he departed from the borders of Tyre and Sidon, and came to the sea of Galilee, through the middle of the region of Decapolis. **32** They brought to him one who was deaf and had an impediment in his speech. They begged him to lay his hand on him. **33** He took him aside from the multitude, privately, and put his fingers into his ears, and he spat, and touched his tongue. **34** Looking up to heaven, he sighed, and said to him, "Ephphatha!" that is, "Be opened!" **35** Immediately his ears were opened, and the impediment of his tongue was released, and he spoke clearly. **36** He commanded them that they should tell no one, but the more he commanded them, so much the more widely they proclaimed it. **37** They were astonished beyond measure, saying, "He has done all things well. He makes even the deaf hear, and the mute speak!"

CHAPTER 8

Jesus feeds a multitude of four thousand people with only seven loaves and a few small fish. The Pharisees question Jesus and ask for a sign from heaven to test him, but Jesus says that no sign will be given. In Bethsaida, Jesus lays his hands on a blind man's eyes and the man's sight is restored. Jesus asks his disciples who they think he is and Peter says "You are the Christ." Jesus then gives the first prophecy of his own death and resurrection.

Those who had eaten were about four thousand. Mark 8:9

The Miracle of Christ Healing the Blind

El Greco

c. 1570

This dramatic and vividly colored painting shows Jesus anointing the eyes of a blind man from Bethsaida to restore his sight. The four Gospels of the New Testament contain several stories of Jesus healing the blind, but this particular one only appears in the Gospel of Mark.

They brought a blind man to him, and begged him to touch him. He took hold of the blind man by the hand, and brought him out of the village. When he had spit on his eyes, and laid his hands on him, he asked him if he saw anything.

Mark 8:22–23

I n those days, when there was a very great multitude, and they had nothing to eat, Jesus called his disciples to himself, and said to them, ² "I have compassion on the multitude, because they have stayed with me now three days, and have nothing to eat. ³ If I send them away fasting to their home, they will faint on the way, for some of them have come a long way."

⁴ His disciples answered him, "From where could one satisfy these people with bread here in a deserted place?"

⁵ He asked them, "How many loaves do you have?"

They said, "Seven."

⁶ He commanded the multitude to sit down on the ground, and he took the seven loaves. Having given thanks, he broke them, and gave them to his disciples to serve, and they served the multitude. ⁷ They had a few small fish. Having blessed them, he said to serve these also. ⁸ They ate, and were filled. They took up seven baskets of broken pieces that were left over. ⁹ Those who had eaten were about four thousand. Then he sent them away.

¹⁰ Immediately he entered into the boat with his disciples, and came into the region of Dalmanutha. ¹¹ The Pharisees came out and began to question him, seeking from him a sign from heaven, and testing him. ¹² He sighed deeply in his spirit, and said, "Why does this generation seek a sign? Most certainly I tell you, no sign will be given to this generation."

¹³ He left them, and again entering into the boat, departed to the other side. ¹⁴ They forgot to take bread; and they did not have more than one loaf in the boat with them. ¹⁵ He warned them, saying, "Take heed: beware of the yeast of the Pharisees and the yeast of Herod."

¹⁶ They reasoned with one another, saying, "It's because we have no bread."

¹⁷ Jesus, perceiving it, said to them, "Why do you reason that it's because you have no bread? Don't you perceive yet, nor understand? Is your heart still hardened? ¹⁸ Having eyes, don't you see? Having ears, don't you hear? Don't you remember? ¹⁹ When I broke the five loaves among the five thousand, how many baskets full of broken pieces did you take up?"

They told him, "Twelve."

²⁰ "When the seven loaves fed the four thousand, how many baskets full of broken pieces did you take up?"

They told him, "Seven."

²¹ He asked them, "Don't you understand, yet?"

²² He came to Bethsaida. They brought a blind man to him, and begged him to touch him. ²³ He took hold of the blind man by the hand, and brought him out of the village. When he had spit on his eyes, and laid his hands on him, he asked him if he saw anything.

²⁴ He looked up, and said, "I see men; for I see them like trees walking."

²⁵ Then again he laid his hands on his eyes. He looked intently, and was restored, and saw everyone clearly. ²⁶ He sent him away to his house, saying, "Don't enter into the village, nor tell anyone in the village."

²⁷ Jesus went out, with his disciples, into the villages of Caesarea Philippi. On the way he asked his disciples, "Who do men say that I am?"

²⁸ They told him, "John the Baptist, and others say Elijah, but others: one of the prophets."

²⁹ He said to them, "But who do you say that I am?"

Peter answered, "You are the Christ [*or Messiah*]."

³⁰ He commanded them that they should tell no one about him. ³¹ He began to teach them that the Son of Man must suffer many things, and be rejected by the elders, the chief priests, and the scribes, and be killed, and after three days rise again. ³² He spoke to them openly. Peter took him, and began to rebuke him. ³³ But he, turning around, and seeing his disciples, rebuked Peter, and said, "Get behind me, Satan! For you have in mind not the things of God, but the things of men."

³⁴ He called the multitude to himself with his disciples, and said to them, "Whoever wants to come after me, let him deny himself, and take up his cross, and follow me. ³⁵ For whoever wants to save his life will lose it; and whoever will lose his life for my sake and the sake of the Good News will save it. ³⁶ For what does it profit a man, to gain the whole world, and forfeit his life? ³⁷ For what will a man give in exchange for his life? ³⁸ For whoever will be ashamed of me and of my words in this adulterous and sinful generation, the Son of Man also will be ashamed of him, when he comes in his Father's glory, with the holy angels."

Get Thee Behind Me, Satan

James Tissot
1886–94

When Jesus prophesied his own death and resurrection to the disciples, Peter rebuked him—people believed that the Messiah would be a glorious warrior, not someone who would be subjected to suffering and humiliation. This watercolor from *The Life of Our Lord Jesus Christ*, a series of 350 illustrations of the Gospels, shows Jesus telling Peter that he is speaking from man's viewpoint, not God's.

CHAPTER 9

Jesus takes the disciples Peter, James, and John up onto a mountain, where they witness his transfiguration—a radiant Jesus is joined by Elijah and Moses, and a voice from a cloud calls Jesus "my beloved Son." On their return, Jesus cures an epileptic boy and prophesies his own death and resurrection for a second time. Back at Capernaum, Jesus continues teaching the disciples and gives them strong warnings against sin.

Elijah and Moses appeared...and they were talking with Jesus. Mark 9:4

He said to them, "Most certainly I tell you, there are some standing here who will in no way taste death until they see God's Kingdom come with power."

² After six days Jesus took with him Peter, James, and John, and brought them up onto a high mountain privately by themselves, and he was changed into another form in front of them. ³ His clothing became glistening, exceedingly white, like snow, such as no launderer on earth can whiten them. ⁴ Elijah and Moses appeared to them, and they were talking with Jesus.

⁵ Peter answered Jesus, "Rabbi, it is good for us to be here. Let's make three tents: one for you, one for Moses, and one for Elijah." ⁶ For he did not know what to say, for they were very afraid.

⁷ A cloud came, overshadowing them, and a voice came out of the cloud, "This is my beloved Son. Listen to him."

⁸ Suddenly looking around, they saw no one with them any more, except Jesus only.

⁹ As they were coming down from the mountain, he commanded them that they should tell no one what things they had seen, until after the Son of Man had risen from the dead. ¹⁰ They kept this saying to themselves, questioning what the "rising from the dead" meant.

¹¹ They asked him, saying, "Why do the scribes say that Elijah must come first?"

¹² He said to them, "Elijah indeed comes first, and restores all things. How is it written about the Son of Man, that he should suffer many things and be despised? ¹³ But I tell you that Elijah has come, and they have also done to him whatever they wanted to, even as it is written about him."

¹⁴ Coming to the disciples, he saw a great multitude around them, and scribes questioning them. ¹⁵ Immediately all the multitude, when they saw him, were greatly amazed, and running to him greeted him. ¹⁶ He asked the scribes, "What are you asking them?"

¹⁷ One of the multitude answered, "Teacher, I brought to you my son, who has a mute spirit; ¹⁸ and wherever it seizes him, it throws him down, and he foams at the mouth, and grinds his teeth, and wastes away. I asked your disciples to cast it out, and they weren't able."

¹⁹ He answered him, "Unbelieving generation, how long shall I be with you? How long shall I bear with you? Bring him to me."

²⁰ They brought him to him, and when he saw him, immediately the spirit convulsed him, and he fell on the ground, wallowing and foaming at the mouth.

²¹ He asked his father, "How long has it been since this has come to him?"

He said, "From childhood. ²² Often it has cast him both into the fire and into the water, to destroy him. But if you can do anything, have compassion on us, and help us."

²³ Jesus said to him, "If you can believe, all things are possible to him who believes."

²⁴ Immediately the father of the child cried out with tears, "I believe. Help my unbelief!"

²⁵ When Jesus saw that a multitude came running together, he rebuked the unclean spirit, saying to him, "You mute and deaf spirit, I command you, come out of him, and never enter him again!"

²⁶ Having cried out, and convulsed greatly, it came out of him. The boy became like one dead; so much that most of them said, "He is dead." ²⁷ But Jesus took him by the hand, and raised him up; and he arose.

The Transfiguration

Raphael
1516–20

This final painting by Renaissance artist Raphael combines two consecutive stories. Christ, transfigured into a radiant form, floats between the Old Testament figures of Moses and Elijah, with the disciples James, Peter, and John on the mountain-top below. In the lower half of the painting the other disciples try to heal a possessed boy (suffering from epilepsy), but cannot do so.

The Healing of the Epileptic

Károly Markó the Younger

19TH CENTURY

On the right, Jesus stands in front of Peter, James, and John, having just come down from the mountain after his transfiguration. On the left, a crowd of people surround a boy possessed by an unclean spirit—that is, suffering from epilepsy—as the boy's father kneels before Jesus and asks him to heal his son. Jesus is shown raising his right hand and ordering the spirit to leave.

"You mute and deaf spirit, I command you, come out of him, and never enter him again!" Having cried out, and convulsed greatly, it came out of him. The boy became like one dead; so much that most of them said, "He is dead." But Jesus took him by the hand, and raised him up; and he arose.

Mark 9:25–27

28 When he had come into the house, his disciples asked him privately, "Why couldn't we cast it out?" **29** He said to them, "This kind can come out by nothing, except by prayer and fasting."

30 They went out from there, and passed through Galilee. He did not want anyone to know it. **31** For he was teaching his disciples, and said to them, "The Son of Man is being handed over to the hands of men, and they will kill him; and when he is killed, on the third day he will rise again."

32 But they did not understand the saying, and were afraid to ask him.

33 He came to Capernaum, and when he was in the house he asked them, "What were you arguing among yourselves on the way?"

34 But they were silent, for they had disputed one with another on the way about who was the greatest.

35 He sat down, and called the twelve; and he said to them, "If any man wants to be first, he shall be last of all, and servant of all." **36** He took a little child, and set him in the middle of them. Taking him in his arms, he said to them, **37** "Whoever receives one such little child in my name, receives me, and whoever receives me, doesn't receive me, but him who sent me."

38 John said to him, "Teacher, we saw someone who doesn't follow us casting out demons in your name; and we forbade him, because he doesn't follow us."

39 But Jesus said, "Don't forbid him, for there is no one who will do a mighty work in my name, and be able quickly to speak evil of me. **40** For whoever is not against us is on our side. **41** For whoever will give you a cup of water to drink in my name, because you are Christ's, most certainly I tell you, he will in no way lose his reward. **42** Whoever will cause one of these little ones who believe in me to stumble, it would be better for him if he were thrown into the sea with a millstone hung around his neck. **43** If your hand causes you to stumble, cut it off. It is better for you to enter into life maimed, rather than having your two hands to go into Gehenna [*or Hell*], into the unquenchable fire, **44** 'where their worm doesn't die, and the fire is not quenched.' [*Some manuscripts omit verses 44 and 46, which are identical to verse 48.*] **45** If your foot causes you to stumble, cut it off. It is better for you to enter into life lame, rather than having your two feet to be cast into Gehenna, into the fire that will never be quenched **46** 'where their worm doesn't die, and the fire is not quenched.' **47** If your eye causes you to stumble, cast it out. It is better for you to enter into God's Kingdom with one eye, rather than having two eyes to be cast into the Gehenna of fire, **48** 'where their worm doesn't die, and the fire is not quenched.' **49** For everyone will be salted with fire, and every sacrifice will be seasoned with salt. **50** Salt is good, but if the salt has lost its saltiness, with what will you season it? Have salt in yourselves, and be at peace with one another."

CHAPTER 10

Jesus denounces divorce, blesses children, and advises renouncing worldly riches in return for heavenly rewards. He prophesies his death and resurrection for the third time. When James and John ask to sit on either side of Jesus when he is glorified, the other disciples are indignant. Jesus warns them all against wanting to be greater than others and says that he himself has come to serve, not be served. When leaving Jericho, Jesus gives the blind beggar Bartimaeus his sight.

He received his sight, and followed Jesus on the way: Mark 10:52

Jesus Blessing the Children

Lorin de Chartres Workshops
c. 1900–10
This stained-glass window in the Church
of Saint-Antoine de Padoue in Paris, France,
depicts the story of Jesus blessing the children.

*"Most certainly I tell you, whoever will not receive God's
Kingdom like a little child, he will in no way enter into it."*

Mark 10:15

He arose from there and came into the borders of Judea and beyond the Jordan. Multitudes came together to him again. As he usually did, he was again teaching them. ² Pharisees came to him testing him, and asked him, "Is it lawful for a man to divorce his wife?"

³ He answered, "What did Moses command you?"

⁴ They said, "Moses allowed a certificate of divorce to be written, and to divorce her."

⁵ But Jesus said to them, "For your hardness of heart, he wrote you this commandment. ⁶ But from the beginning of the creation, God made them male and female. ⁷ For this cause a man will leave his father and mother, and will join to his wife, ⁸ and the two will become one flesh, so that they are no longer two, but one flesh. ⁹ What therefore God has joined together, let no man separate."

¹⁰ In the house, his disciples asked him again about the same matter. ¹¹ He said to them, "Whoever divorces his wife, and marries another, commits adultery against her. ¹² If a woman herself divorces her husband, and marries another, she commits adultery."

¹³ They were bringing to him little children, that he should touch them, but the disciples rebuked those who were bringing them. ¹⁴ But when Jesus saw it, he was moved with indignation, and said to them, "Allow the little children to come to me! Don't forbid them, for God's Kingdom belongs to such as these. ¹⁵ Most certainly I tell you, whoever will not receive God's Kingdom like a little child, he will in no way enter into it." ¹⁶ He took them in his arms, and blessed them, laying his hands on them.

¹⁷ As he was going out into the way, one ran to him, knelt before him, and asked him, "Good Teacher, what shall I do that I may inherit eternal life?"

¹⁸ Jesus said to him, "Why do you call me good? No one is good except one—God. ¹⁹ You know the commandments: 'Do not murder,' 'Do not commit adultery,' 'Do not steal,' 'Do not give false testimony,' 'Do not defraud,' 'Honor your father and mother.'"

²⁰ He said to him, "Teacher, I have observed all these things from my youth."

²¹ Jesus looking at him loved him, and said to him, "One thing you lack. Go, sell whatever you have, and give to the poor, and you will have treasure in heaven; and come, follow me, taking up the cross."

²² But his face fell at that saying, and he went away sorrowful, for he was one who had great possessions. ²³ Jesus looked around,

and said to his disciples, "How difficult it is for those who have riches to enter into God's Kingdom!"

24 The disciples were amazed at his words. But Jesus answered again, "Children, how hard is it for those who trust in riches to enter into God's Kingdom! 25 It is easier for a camel to go through the eye of a needle than for a rich man to enter into God's Kingdom."

26 They were exceedingly astonished, saying to him, "Then who can be saved?"

27 Jesus, looking at them, said, "With men it is impossible, but not with God, for all things are possible with God."

28 Peter began to tell him, "Behold, we have left all, and have followed you."

29 Jesus said, "Most certainly I tell you, there is no one who has left house, or brothers, or sisters, or father, or mother, or wife, or children, or land, for my sake, and for the sake of the Good News, 30 but he will receive one hundred times more now in this time, houses, brothers, sisters, mothers, children, and land, with persecutions; and in the age to come eternal life. 31 But many who are first will be last; and the last first."

32 They were on the way, going up to Jerusalem; and Jesus was going in front of them, and they were amazed; and those who followed were afraid. He again took the twelve, and began to tell them the things that were going to happen to him. 33 "Behold, we are going up to Jerusalem. The Son of Man will be delivered to the chief priests and the scribes. They will condemn him to death, and will deliver him to the Gentiles. 34 They will mock him, spit on him, scourge him, and kill him. On the third day he will rise again."

Christ Healing the Blind Man on the Road to Jericho

Petrus Norbertus van Reysschoot
18TH CENTURY

Jesus healed a blind beggar named Bartimaeus as he was leaving Jericho. Bartimaeus is one of the few people miraculously healed by Jesus who is identified by name in the Gospels.

35 James and John, the sons of Zebedee, came near to him, saying, "Teacher, we want you to do for us whatever we will ask."

36 He said to them, "What do you want me to do for you?"

37 They said to him, "Grant to us that we may sit, one at your right hand, and one at your left hand, in your glory."

38 But Jesus said to them, "You don't know what you are asking. Are you able to drink the cup that I drink, and to be baptized with the baptism that I am baptized with?"

39 They said to him, "We are able."

Jesus said to them, "You shall indeed drink the cup that I drink, and you shall be baptized with the baptism that I am baptized with; 40 but to sit at my right hand and at my left hand is not mine to give, but for whom it has been prepared."

41 When the ten heard it, they began to be indignant toward James and John.

42 Jesus summoned them, and said to them, "You know that they who are recognized as rulers over the nations lord it over them, and their great ones exercise authority over them. 43 But it shall not be so among you, but whoever wants to become great among you shall be your servant. 44 Whoever of you wants to become first among you, shall be bondservant of all. 45 For the Son of Man also came not to be served, but to serve, and to give his life as a ransom for many."

46 They came to Jericho. As he went out from Jericho, with his disciples and a great multitude, the son of Timaeus, Bartimaeus, a blind beggar, was sitting by the road. 47 When he heard that it was Jesus the Nazarene, he began to cry out, and say, "Jesus, you son of David, have mercy on me!" 48 Many rebuked him, that he should be quiet, but he cried out much more, "You son of David, have mercy on me!"

49 Jesus stood still, and said, "Call him."

They called the blind man, saying to him, "Cheer up! Get up. He is calling you!"

50 He, casting away his cloak, sprang up, and came to Jesus.

51 Jesus asked him, "What do you want me to do for you?"

The blind man said to him, "Rabbi, that I may see again."

52 Jesus said to him, "Go your way. Your faith has made you well." Immediately he received his sight, and followed Jesus on the way.

CHAPTER 11

Jesus enters Jerusalem riding a donkey, with crowds of people spreading garments and branches on the ground before him. They proclaim him to be coming in the name of the Lord. Jesus looks for fruit on a fig tree, finds none, and curses the tree. When the tree is later found withered, Jesus talks about the power of prayer. Jesus finds people transacting business in the Temple in Jerusalem and throws them out, declaring it to be a place of prayer. The chief priests and scribes challenge Jesus' authority to do so and continue to plot to destroy him.

"Isn't it written, 'My house will be called a house of prayer…?'" Mark 11:17

They brought the young donkey to Jesus, and threw their garments on it, and Jesus sat on it…Those who went in front, and those who followed, cried out, "Hosanna! Blessed is he who comes in the name of the Lord! Blessed is the kingdom of our father David that is coming in the name of the Lord! Hosanna in the highest!"

Mark 11:7–10

When they came near to Jerusalem, to Bethsphage and Bethany, at the Mount of Olives, he sent two of his disciples, **2** and said to them, "Go your way into the village that is opposite you. Immediately as you enter into it, you will find a young donkey tied, on which no one has sat. Untie him, and bring him. **3** If anyone asks you, 'Why are you doing this?' say, 'The Lord needs him'; and immediately he will send him back here."

4 They went away, and found a young donkey tied at the door outside in the open street, and they untied him. **5** Some of those who stood there asked them, "What are you doing, untying the young donkey?" **6** They said to them just as Jesus had said, and they let them go.

7 They brought the young donkey to Jesus, and threw their garments on it, and Jesus sat on it. **8** Many spread their garments on the way, and others were cutting down branches from the trees, and spreading them on the road. **9** Those who went in front, and those who followed, cried out, "Hosanna! Blessed is he who comes in the name of the Lord! [*Meaning "save us," hosanna was used as an exclamation of praise.*] **10** Blessed is the kingdom of our father David that is coming in the name of the Lord! Hosanna in the highest!"

11 Jesus entered into the temple in Jerusalem. When he had looked around at everything, it being now evening, he went out to Bethany with the twelve.

12 The next day, when they had come out from Bethany, he was hungry. **13** Seeing a fig tree afar off having leaves, he came to see if perhaps he might find anything on it. When he came to it, he found nothing but leaves, for it was not the season for figs. **14** Jesus told it, "May no one ever eat fruit from you again!" and his disciples heard it.

15 They came to Jerusalem, and Jesus entered into the temple, and began to throw out those who sold and those who bought in the temple, and overthrew the tables of the money changers, and the seats of those who sold the doves. **16** He would not allow anyone to carry a container through the temple. **17** He taught, saying to them, "Isn't it written, 'My house will be called a house of prayer for all the nations?' But you have made it a den of robbers!"

18 The chief priests and the scribes heard it, and sought how they might destroy him. For they feared him, because all the multitude was astonished at his teaching.

19 When evening came, he went out of the city. **20** As they passed by in the morning, they saw the fig tree withered away from the roots. **21** Peter, remembering, said to him, "Rabbi, look! The fig tree which you cursed has withered away."

22 Jesus answered them, "Have faith in God. **23** For most certainly I tell you, whoever

Christ Entering Jerusalem

Cristoforo de Predis
1476

This image from the *Predis Codex*, a bound collection of the artist's miniature biblical paintings, shows Jesus entering Jerusalem on a donkey. Onlookers spread garments and branches on the road before Jesus, and hailed him as coming in the name of the Lord. This triumphal entrance is celebrated by Christians as Palm Sunday, a week before Easter Sunday.

may tell this mountain, 'Be taken up and cast into the sea,' and doesn't doubt in his heart, but believes that what he says is happening; he shall have whatever he says. **24** Therefore I tell you, all things whatever you pray and ask for, believe that you have received them, and you shall have them. **25** Whenever you stand praying, forgive, if you have anything against anyone; so that your Father, who is in heaven, may also forgive you your transgressions. **26** But if you do not forgive, neither will your Father in heaven forgive your transgressions."

27 They came again to Jerusalem, and as he was walking in the temple, the chief priests, and the scribes, and the elders came to him, **28** and they began saying to him, "By what authority do you do these things? Or who gave you this authority to do these things?"

29 Jesus said to them, "I will ask you one question. Answer me, and I will tell you by what authority I do these things. **30** The baptism of John—was it from heaven, or from men? Answer me."

31 They reasoned with themselves, saying, "If we should say, 'From heaven'; he will say, 'Why then did you not believe him?' **32** If we should say, 'From men' "—they feared the people, for all held John to really be a prophet. **33** They answered Jesus, "We don't know."

Jesus said to them, "Neither do I tell you by what authority I do these things."

Christ Driving the Traders from the Temple

El Greco

c. 1600

In the time of Jesus various commercial activities took place in the Temple in Jerusalem. Traders sold livestock for sacrifices, and money changers exchanged money into the required currency for paying the annual Temple tax. Jesus, enraged that these transactions were taking place within the Temple precinct, threw out the traders, saying that they had made the Temple a den of thieves. Here, Jesus stands at the center of the painting, with the traders on the left and the disciples on the right.

CHAPTER 12

Jesus tells the parable of the vineyard, in which the tenant farmers kill the owner's representatives in order to keep the harvest for themselves. The priests and scribes perceive the parable to be a message against themselves. They question Jesus to try to trap him with words—asking whether they should pay taxes to Caesar, about life after death, and which is the greatest commandment. When Jesus sees a poor widow giving two small brass coins to the treasury, he says that she is actually giving a greater amount than rich people who give more money.

"Render to Caesar the things that are Caesar's..." Mark 12:17

He began to speak to them in parables. "A man planted a vineyard, put a hedge around it, dug a pit for the wine press, built a tower, rented it out to a farmer, and went into another country. **2** When it was time, he sent a servant to the farmer to get from the farmer his share of the fruit of the vineyard. **3** They took him, beat him, and sent him away empty. **4** Again, he sent another servant to them; and they threw stones at him, wounded him in the head, and sent him away shamefully treated. **5** Again he sent another; and they killed him; and many others, beating some, and killing some. **6** Therefore still having one, his beloved son, he sent him last to them, saying, 'They will respect my son.' **7** But those farmers said among themselves, 'This is the heir. Come, let's kill him, and the inheritance will be ours.' **8** They took him, killed him, and cast him out of the vineyard. **9** What therefore will the lord of the vineyard do? He will come and destroy the farmers, and will give the vineyard to others. **10** Haven't you read this Scripture:

'The stone which the builders rejected,
    this was made the cornerstone.
11 This was the Lord's doing,
    and it is marvelous in our eyes'?"

12 They tried to seize him, but they feared the multitude; for they perceived that he spoke the parable against them. They left him, and went away. **13** They sent some of the Pharisees and of the Herodians to him, that they might trap him with words. **14** When they had come, they asked him, "Teacher, we know that you are honest, and don't defer to anyone; for you aren't partial to anyone, but truly teach the way of God. Is it lawful to pay taxes to Caesar, or not? **15** Shall we give, or shall we not give?"

But he, knowing their hypocrisy, said to them, "Why do you test me? Bring me a denarius, that I may see it."

16 They brought it.

He said to them, "Whose is this image and inscription?"

They said to him, "Caesar's."

17 Jesus answered them, "Render to Caesar the things that are Caesar's, and to God the things that are God's."

They marveled greatly at him.

18 There came to him Sadducees, who say that there is no resurrection. They asked him, saying, **19** "Teacher, Moses wrote to us, 'If a man's brother dies, and leaves a wife behind him, and leaves no children, that his brother should take his wife, and raise up offspring for his brother.' **20** There were seven brothers. The first took a wife, and dying left no offspring. **21** The second took her, and died, leaving no children behind him. The third likewise; **22** and the seven took her and left no children. Last of all the woman also died. **23** In the resurrection, when they rise, whose wife will she be of them? For the seven had her as a wife."

PREVIOUS PAGE: **The Parable of the Bad Vintners**

Marten van Valckenborch
c. 1580–90

In the foreground, two pairs of tenant farmers are shown harvesting the crop. In a field behind them the son of the vineyard owner requests the owner's share of the crop. In the lower right corner servants, also sent by the owner to request his share, are being beaten by the tenants, while work in the winepress carries on behind them.

OPPOSITE: **The Tribute Money**

Anthony van Dyck
c. 1625

The Pharisees and Herodians tried to trap Jesus by asking whether Jews should pay taxes to the Roman authorities—taking either side in the argument would be controversial. In this painting the man on the right holds out a coin bearing the image of Caesar and Jesus avoids the trap by responding that they should "Render to Caesar the things that are Caesar's, and to God the things that are God's" (Genesis 12:17).

The Widow's Mite

Italian School

EARLY 6TH CENTURY

This glittering Byzantine mosaic in the Basilica of Sant'Apollinare Nuovo in Ravenna, Italy, depicts the story of the poor widow who gives two small brass coins to the treasury. Jesus can be seen telling his disciples that the widow is in fact making a far more generous donation than richer people, since she is giving all that she has to live on.

"Most certainly I tell you, this poor widow gave more than all those who are giving into the treasury; for they all gave out of their abundance, but she, out of her poverty, gave all that she had to live on."

Mark 12:43–44

24 Jesus answered them, "Isn't this because you are mistaken, not knowing the Scriptures, nor the power of God? 25 For when they will rise from the dead, they neither marry, nor are given in marriage, but are like angels in heaven. 26 But about the dead being raised; haven't you read in the book of Moses, about the Bush, how God spoke to him, saying, 'I am the God of Abraham, the God of Isaac, and the God of Jacob'? 27 He is not the God of the dead, but of the living. You are therefore badly mistaken."

28 One of the scribes came, and heard them questioning together. Knowing that he had answered them well, asked him, "Which commandment is the greatest of all?"

29 Jesus answered, "The greatest is, 'Hear, Israel, the Lord our God, the Lord is one: 30 you shall love the Lord your God with all your heart, and with all your soul, and with all your mind, and with all your strength.' This is the first commandment. 31 The second is like this, 'You shall love your neighbor as yourself.' There is no other commandment greater than these."

32 The scribe said to him, "Truly, teacher, you have said well that he is one, and there is none other but he, 33 and to love him with all the heart, and with all the understanding, with all the soul, and with all the strength, and to love his neighbor as himself, is more important than all whole burnt offerings and sacrifices."

34 When Jesus saw that he answered wisely, he said to him, "You are not far from God's Kingdom."

No one dared ask him any question after that. 35 Jesus responded, as he taught in the temple, "How is it that the scribes say that the Christ is the son of David? 36 For David himself, inspired by the Holy Spirit, said:
'The Lord said to my Lord,
    "Sit at my right hand,
    until I make your enemies
        the footstool of your feet."'
37 Therefore David himself calls him Lord, so how can he be his son?"

The common people heard him gladly. 38 In his teaching he said to them, "Beware of the scribes, who like to walk in long robes, and to get greetings in the marketplaces, 39 and the best seats in the synagogues, and the best places at feasts: 40 those who devour widows' houses, and for a pretense make long prayers. These will receive greater condemnation."

41 Jesus sat down opposite the treasury, and saw how the multitude cast money into the treasury. Many who were rich cast in much. 42 A poor widow came, and she cast in two small brass coins, which equal a quadrans coin [*the brass coins were called lepta (widow's mites) and were worth half a quadrans each; a quadrans was equivalent to about one day's wages for an agricultural laborer*]. 43 He called his disciples to himself, and said to them, "Most certainly I tell you, this poor widow gave more than all those who are giving into the treasury, 44 for they all gave out of their abundance, but she, out of her poverty, gave all that she had to live on."

CHAPTER 13

Jesus foretells the Sack of Jerusalem and the destruction of the Temple. He describes terrible disasters that will befall the world, but tells the disciples not to be troubled because these things have to happen before he returns in his glory. Jesus says that the disciples must go out and preach to all nations, and trust in the Holy Spirit when they suffer for this. He warns that false christs and prophets will lead many astray, and urges them to be vigilant because not even Jesus can foretell when these things will happen.

The Good News must first be preached to all the nations. Mark 13:10

Jesus Among the False Prophets

Liberale da Verona

15TH CENTURY

Jesus warned the disciples to beware of the false prophets that would arise and lead people astray. This illuminated letter, depicting Jesus among the false prophets, is from a gradual—a book of chants sung during mass.

As he went out of the temple, one of his disciples said to him, "Teacher, look at the great stones and buildings!" 2 Jesus said to him, "Do you see these great buildings? There will not be left here one stone on another, which will not be thrown down."

3 As he sat on the Mount of Olives opposite the temple, Peter, James, John, and Andrew asked him privately, 4 "Tell us, when will these things be? What is the sign that these things are all about to be fulfilled?"

5 Jesus, answering, began to tell them, "Be careful that no one leads you astray. 6 For many will come in my name, saying, 'I am he!' and will lead many astray.

7 "When you hear of wars and rumors of wars, don't be troubled. For those must happen, but the end is not yet. 8 For nation will rise against nation, and kingdom against kingdom. There will be earthquakes in various places. There will be famines and troubles. These things are the beginning of birth pains. 9 But watch yourselves, for they will deliver you up to councils. You will be beaten in synagogues. You will stand before rulers and kings for my sake, for a testimony to them. 10 The Good News must first be preached to all the nations. 11 When they lead you away and deliver you up, don't be anxious beforehand, or premeditate what you will say, but say whatever will be given you in that hour. For it is not you who speak, but the Holy Spirit.

12 "Brother will deliver up brother to death, and the father his child. Children will rise up against parents, and cause them to be put to death. 13 You will be hated by all men for my name's sake, but he who endures to the end, the same will be saved. 14 But when you see the abomination of desolation, spoken of by Daniel the prophet, standing where it ought not (let the reader understand), then let those who are in Judea flee to the mountains, 15 and let him who is on the housetop not go down, nor enter in, to take anything out of his house. 16 Let him who is in the field not return back to take his cloak. 17 But woe to those who are with child and to those who nurse babies in those days! 18 Pray that your flight won't be in the winter. 19 For in those days there will be oppression, such as there has not been the like from the beginning of the creation which God created until now, and never will be. 20 Unless the Lord had shortened the days, no flesh would have been saved; but for the sake of the chosen ones, whom he picked out, he shortened the days. 21 Then if anyone tells you, 'Look, here is the Christ!' or, 'Look, there!' don't believe it. 22 For there will arise false christs and false prophets, who will show signs and wonders, that they may lead astray, if possible, even the chosen ones. 23 But you watch.

"Behold, I have told you all things beforehand. 24 But in those days, after that oppression, the sun will be darkened, the moon will not give its light, 25 the stars will be falling from the sky, and the powers that are in the heavens will be shaken. 26 Then they will see the Son of Man coming in clouds with great power and glory. 27 Then he will send out his angels, and will gather together his chosen ones from the four winds, from the ends of the earth to the ends of the sky.

28 "Now from the fig tree, learn this parable. When the branch has now become tender, and produces its leaves, you know that the summer is near; 29 even so you also, when you see these things coming to pass, know that it is near, at the doors. 30 Most certainly I say to you, this generation will not pass away until all these things happen. 31 Heaven and earth will pass away, but my words will not pass away. 32 But of that day or that hour no one knows, not even the angels in heaven, nor the Son, but only the Father. 33 Watch, keep alert, and pray; for you don't know when the time is.

34 "It is like a man, traveling to another country, having left his house, and given authority to his servants, and to each one his work, and also commanded the doorkeeper to keep watch. 35 Watch therefore, for you don't know when the lord of the house is coming, whether at evening, or at midnight, or when the rooster crows, or in the morning; 36 lest coming suddenly he might find you sleeping. 37 What I tell you, I tell all: Watch."

CHAPTER 14

A woman anoints Jesus and he commends her for doing what she can before his burial. At a Passover meal—the Last Supper—Jesus predicts that one of the disciples will betray him. During the meal, he gives thanks and blesses the bread and wine—an event that Christians reenact in the sacrament of the Eucharist. Jesus goes to Gethsemane to pray, asking to be spared the ordeal to come. Judas arrives, identifies Jesus with a kiss, and Jesus is arrested and accused of blasphemy. Peter denies knowing Jesus three times, fulfilling an earlier prediction.

"Whomever I will kiss, that is he. Seize him…" Mark 14:44

Anointing of Jesus

Flemish School

16TH CENTURY

This stained-glass panel depicts the story of the woman pouring a jar of expensive ointment over Jesus' head during a meal. Some of those present complained about the waste, but Jesus said that she was anointing him before his burial. Although often identified as Mary Magdalene, only John's Gospel names the woman—Mary of Bethany, not Mary Magdalene.

"She has done what she could. She has anointed my body beforehand for burying. Most certainly I tell you, wherever this Good News may be preached throughout the whole world, that which this woman has done will also be spoken of for a memorial of her."

Mark 14:8–9

It was now two days before the feast of the Passover and the unleavened bread, and the chief priests and the scribes sought how they might seize him by deception, and kill him. **2** For they said, "Not during the feast, because there might be a riot of the people."

3 While he was at Bethany, in the house of Simon the leper, as he sat at the table, a woman came having an alabaster jar of ointment of pure nard—very costly. She broke the jar, and poured it over his head. **4** But there were some who were indignant among themselves, saying, "Why has this ointment been wasted? **5** For this might have been sold for more than three hundred denarii [*300 denarii was about a year's wages for an agricultural laborer*], and given to the poor." They grumbled against her.

6 But Jesus said, "Leave her alone. Why do you trouble her? She has done a good work for me. **7** For you always have the poor with you, and whenever you want to, you can do them good; but you will not always have me. **8** She has done what she could. She has anointed my body beforehand for burying. **9** Most certainly I tell you, wherever this Good News may be preached throughout the whole world, that which this woman has done will also be spoken of for a memorial of her."

10 Judas Iscariot, who was one of the twelve, went away to the chief priests, that he might deliver him to them. **11** They, when they heard it, were glad, and promised to give him money. He sought how he might conveniently deliver him. **12** On the first day of unleavened bread, when they sacrificed the Passover, his disciples asked him, "Where do you want us to go and prepare that you may eat the Passover?"

13 He sent two of his disciples, and said to them, "Go into the city, and there you will meet a man carrying a pitcher of water. Follow him, **14** and wherever he enters in, tell the master of the house, 'The Teacher says, "Where is the guest room, where I may eat the Passover with my disciples?" ' **15** He will himself show you a large upper room furnished and ready. Get ready for us there."

16 His disciples went out, and came into the city, and found things as he had said to them, and they prepared the Passover.

17 When it was evening he came with the twelve. **18** As they sat and were eating, Jesus said, "Most certainly I tell you, one of you will betray me—he who eats with me."

19 They began to be sorrowful, and to ask him one by one, "Surely not I?" And another said, "Surely not I?"

20 He answered them, "It is one of the twelve, he who dips with me in the dish. **21** For the Son of Man goes, even as it is written about him, but woe to that man by whom the Son of Man is betrayed! It would be better for that man if he had not been born."

22 As they were eating, Jesus took bread, and when he had blessed, he broke it, and gave it to them, and said, "Take, eat. This is my body."

23 He took the cup, and when he had given thanks, he gave it to them. They all drank of it. **24** He said to them, "This is my blood of the new covenant, which is poured out for many. **25** Most certainly I tell you, I will no more drink of the fruit of the vine, until that day when I drink it anew in God's Kingdom." **26** When they had sung a hymn, they went out to the Mount of Olives.

27 Jesus said to them, "All of you will be made to stumble because of me tonight, for it is written, 'I will strike the shepherd, and the sheep will be scattered.' **28** However, after I am raised up, I will go before you into Galilee."

29 But Peter said to him, "Although all will stumble, yet I will not."

30 Jesus said to him, "Most certainly I tell you, that you today, even this night, before the rooster crows twice, you will deny me three times."

31 But he spoke all the more, "If I must die with you, I will not deny you." They all said the same thing.

32 They came to a place which was named Gethsemane. He said to his disciples, "Sit here, while I pray." **33** He took with him Peter, James, and John, and began to be greatly troubled and distressed. **34** He said to them, "My soul is exceedingly sorrowful, even to death. Stay here, and watch."

The Last Supper

Jacopo Bassano
1542

This dramatic painting depicts the final meal of Jesus with his twelve disciples. The scene shows the crucial moment when Christ reveals that one of the disciples will betray him.

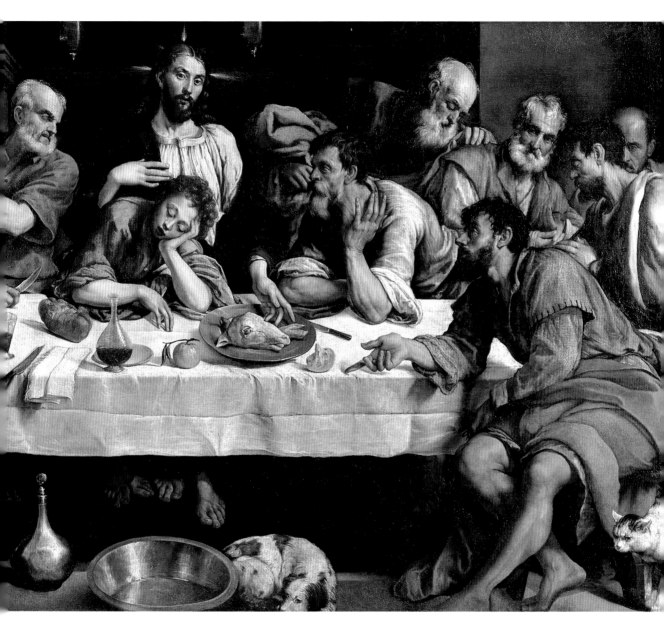

As they sat and were eating, Jesus said, "Most certainly I tell you, one of you will betray me— he who eats with me." They began to be sorrowful, and to ask him one by one, "Surely not I?" And another said, "Surely not I?" He answered them, "It is one of the twelve, he who dips with me in the dish."

Mark 14:18–20

*He said, "Abba, Father, all things are possible to you.
Please remove this cup from me."*

Mark 14:36

35 He went forward a little, and fell on the ground, and prayed that, if it were possible, the hour might pass away from him. 36 He said, "Abba, Father, all things are possible to you. Please remove this cup from me. However, not what I desire, but what you desire."

37 He came and found them sleeping, and said to Peter, "Simon, are you sleeping? Couldn't you watch one hour? 38 Watch and pray, that you may not enter into temptation. The spirit indeed is willing, but the flesh is weak."

39 Again he went away, and prayed, saying the same words. 40 Again he returned, and found them sleeping, for their eyes were very heavy, and they did not know what to answer him. 41 He came the third time, and said to them, "Sleep on now, and take your rest. It is enough. The hour has come. Behold, the Son of Man is betrayed into the hands of sinners. 42 Arise, let us be going. Behold, he who betrays me is at hand."

43 Immediately, while he was still speaking, Judas, one of the twelve, came—and with him a multitude with swords and clubs, from the chief priests, the scribes, and the elders. 44 Now he who betrayed him had given them a sign, saying, "Whomever I will kiss, that is he. Seize him, and lead him away safely." 45 When he had come, immediately he came to him, and said, "Rabbi! Rabbi!" and kissed him. 46 They laid their hands on him, and seized him. 47 But a certain one of those who stood by drew his sword, and struck the servant of the high priest, and cut off his ear.

48 Jesus answered them, "Have you come out, as against a robber, with swords and clubs to seize me? 49 I was daily with you in the temple teaching, and you didn't arrest me. But this is so that the Scriptures might be fulfilled."

50 They all left him, and fled. 51 A certain young man followed him, having a linen cloth thrown around himself, over his naked body. The young men grabbed him, 52 but he left the linen cloth, and fled from them naked. 53 They led Jesus away to the high priest. All the chief priests, the elders, and the scribes came together with him.

54 Peter had followed him from a distance, until he came into the court of the high priest. He was sitting with the officers, and warming himself in the light of the fire. 55 Now the chief priests and the whole council sought witnesses against Jesus to put him to death, and found none. 56 For many gave false testimony against him, and their testimony did not agree with each other. 57 Some stood up, and gave false testimony against him, saying, 58 "We heard him say, 'I will destroy this temple that is made with hands, and in three days I will build another made without hands.'" 59 Even so, their testimony did not agree.

Now he who betrayed him had given them a sign, saying, "Whomever I will kiss, that is he. Seize him, and lead him away safely." When he had come, immediately he came to him, and said, "Rabbi! Rabbi!" and kissed him. They laid their hands on him, and seized him.

Mark 14:44–46

The Kiss of Judas

Giotto di Bondone

c. 1303–05

This scene from the *Life of Christ* fresco cycle in the Scrovegni Chapel in Padua, Italy, shows Judas in a yellow cloak reaching up to kiss Jesus, while all around a crowd brandishes clubs and swords. On the left, one of the disciples can be seen reacting to the moment of betrayal by drawing his sword and cutting off the ear of the high priest's servant.

60 The high priest stood up in the middle, and asked Jesus, "Have you no answer? What is it which these testify against you?" **61** But he stayed quiet, and answered nothing. Again the high priest asked him, "Are you the Christ, the Son of the Blessed?"

62 Jesus said, "I am. You will see the Son of Man sitting at the right hand of Power, and coming with the clouds of the sky."

63 The high priest tore his clothes, and said, "What further need have we of witnesses? **64** You have heard the blasphemy! What do you think?" They all condemned him to be worthy of death. **65** Some began to spit on him, and to cover his face, and to beat him with fists, and to tell him, "Prophesy!" The officers struck him with the palms of their hands.

66 As Peter was in the courtyard below, one of the maids of the high priest came, **67** and seeing Peter warming himself, she looked at him, and said, "You were also with the Nazarene, Jesus!"

68 But he denied it, saying, "I neither know, nor understand what you are saying." He went out on the porch, and the rooster crowed.

69 The maid saw him, and began again to tell those who stood by, "This is one of them." **70** But he again denied it. After a little while again those who stood by said to Peter, "You truly are one of them, for you are a Galilean, and your speech shows it." **71** But he began to curse, and to swear, "I don't know this man of whom you speak!" **72** The rooster crowed the second time. Peter remembered the word, how that Jesus said to him, "Before the rooster crows twice, you will deny me three times." When he thought about that, he wept.

The Denial of St. Peter

Valentin de Boulogne
1620

When Jesus was arrested, Peter followed him to the courtyard of the high priest. In this painting Peter sits at the table on the far left, alongside a maid and a group of guards. The maid asserted that she recognized Peter as an associate of Jesus, but Peter denied this three times, as foretold by Jesus at the Last Supper.

CHAPTER 15

Jesus is delivered to Pilate, the Roman governor of Judea. The chief priests stir up the crowd to demand that Pilate condemn Jesus to crucifixion. Soldiers mock Jesus and crown him with thorns as "King of the Jews." They take Jesus to Golgotha, where he is crucified with a robber on each side of him. Joseph of Arimathaea asks Pilate for Jesus' body. Joseph wraps the body in a linen cloth and lays Jesus in a tomb, with a stone against the door. Mary Magdalene is among the witnesses to the crucifixion and burial.

...and they crucified him. Mark 15:25

Immediately in the morning the chief priests, with the elders and scribes, and the whole council, held a consultation, and bound Jesus, and carried him away, and delivered him up to Pilate. ² Pilate asked him, "Are you the King of the Jews?"

He answered, "So you say."

³ The chief priests accused him of many things. ⁴ Pilate again asked him, "Have you no answer? See how many things they testify against you!"

⁵ But Jesus made no further answer, so that Pilate marveled.

⁶ Now at the feast he used to release to them one prisoner, whom they asked of him. ⁷ There was one called Barabbas, bound with his fellow insurgents, men who in the insurrection had committed murder. ⁸ The multitude, crying aloud, began to ask him to do as he always did for them. ⁹ Pilate answered them, saying, "Do you want me to release to you the King of the Jews?" ¹⁰ For he perceived that for envy the chief priests had delivered him up. ¹¹ But the chief priests stirred up the multitude, that he should release Barabbas to them instead. ¹² Pilate again asked them, "What then should I do to him whom you call the King of the Jews?"

¹³ They cried out again, "Crucify him!"

¹⁴ Pilate said to them, "Why, what evil has he done?"

But they cried out exceedingly, "Crucify him!"

Christ Before Pilate

Duccio di Buoninsegna
1308–11

This panel from the Maesta' of Duccio altarpiece in the Cathedral of Siena, Italy, depicts Jesus flanked by soldiers and being questioned by Pilate after his arrest. Jesus' accusers, the chief priests, stand on the far left, stirring up the crowd to call for Jesus' crucifixion. Although Pilate recognized that the charges against Jesus were borne of envy, he acquiesced to the demand.

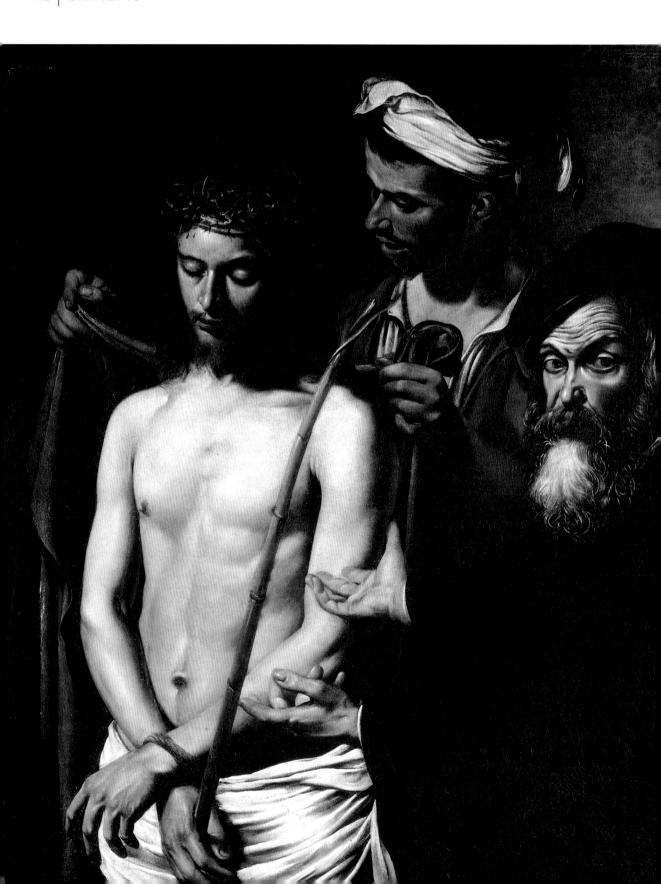

15 Pilate, wishing to please the multitude, released Barabbas to them, and handed over Jesus, when he had flogged him, to be crucified. **16** The soldiers led him away within the court, which is the Praetorium; and they called together the whole cohort. **17** They clothed him with purple, and weaving a crown of thorns, they put it on him. **18** They began to salute him, "Hail, King of the Jews!" **19** They struck his head with a reed, and spat on him, and bowing their knees, did homage to him. **20** When they had mocked him, they took the purple off him, and put his own garments on him. They led him out to crucify him. **21** They compelled one passing by, coming from the country, Simon of Cyrene, the father of Alexander and Rufus, to go with them, that he might bear his cross. **22** They brought him to the place called Golgotha, which is, being interpreted, "The place of a skull." **23** They offered him wine mixed with myrrh to drink, but he did not take it.

24 Crucifying him, they parted his garments among them, casting lots on them, what each should take. **25** It was the third hour [9 A.M.], and they crucified him. **26** The superscription of his accusation was written over him, "THE KING OF THE JEWS." **27** With him they crucified two robbers; one on his right hand, and one on his left. **28** The Scripture was fulfilled, which says, "He was counted with transgressors."

29 Those who passed by blasphemed him, wagging their heads, and saying, "Ha! You

who destroy the temple, and build it in three days, **30** save yourself, and come down from the cross!"

31 Likewise, also the chief priests mocking among themselves with the scribes said, "He saved others. He can't save himself. **32** Let the Christ, the King of Israel, now come down from the cross, that we may see and believe him." Those who were crucified with him also insulted him.

33 When the sixth hour [*noon*] had come, there was darkness over the whole land until the ninth hour. **34** At the ninth hour [*3 P.M.*] Jesus cried with a loud voice, saying, "Eloi, Eloi, lama sabachthani?" which is, being interpreted, "My God, my God, why have you forsaken me?"

35 Some of those who stood by, when they heard it, said, "Behold, he is calling Elijah."

36 One ran, and filling a sponge full of vinegar, put it on a reed, and gave it to him to drink, saying, "Let him be. Let's see whether Elijah comes to take him down."

37 Jesus cried out with a loud voice, and gave up the spirit. **38** The veil of the temple was torn in two from the top to the bottom. **39** When the centurion, who stood by opposite him, saw that he cried out like this and breathed his last, he said, "Truly this man was the Son of God!"

40 There were also women watching from afar, among whom were both Mary Magdalene, and Mary the mother of James the Less and of Joses, and Salome; **41** who, when he was in Galilee, followed him, and served him; and many other women who came up with him to Jerusalem.

42 When evening had now come, because it was the Preparation Day, that is, the day before the Sabbath, **43** Joseph of Arimathaea, a prominent council member who also himself was looking for God's Kingdom, came. He boldly went in to Pilate, and asked for Jesus' body. **44** Pilate marveled if he were already dead; and summoning the centurion, he asked him whether he had been dead long. **45** When he found out from the centurion, he granted the body to Joseph. **46** He bought a linen cloth, and taking him down, wound him in the linen cloth, and laid him in a tomb which had been cut out of a rock. He rolled a stone against the door of the tomb. **47** Mary Magdalene and Mary, the mother of Joses, saw where he was laid.

Ecce Homo (Behold the Man)

Michelangelo Merisi da Caravaggio
c. 1605

After being condemned to death, Jesus was scourged and then mocked by the soldiers, who dressed him in a purple cloak and a crown of thorns, and saluted him as "King of the Jews." The man on the right of the painting is Pilate; the man at the center is one of the soldiers.

ABOVE: **Christ Carrying the Cross**

Hans Holbein the Elder
1494–1500

This image is one of the twelve panels from Holbein's *Gray Passion*, which would originally have adorned an altarpiece. Unusually for an altarpiece, the emotive scenes are painted in a semi-grisaille (monochromatic) palette of gray, ocher, and green.

OPPOSITE: **Christ Between the Two Thieves**

Peter Paul Rubens
c. 1635

Jesus crucified between two thieves, with the women and the Roman centurion who witnessed his death at his feet. Above Jesus' head is the acronym "INRI"— Jesus of Nazareth, King of the Jews.

The Lamentation of Christ

Giotto di Bondone
c. 1303–05

This scene is part of the *Life of Christ* fresco cycle in the Scrovegni Chapel in Padua, Italy. This detail shows several figures mourning over the dead body of Jesus after he is taken down from the cross. The likely identities of three of the haloed figures included in the scene by Giotto are John the Baptist (leaning over on the right), the Virgin Mary (cradling Jesus' head), and Mary Magdalene (holding Jesus' feet).

CHAPTER 16

After the Sabbath, Mary Magdalene and two other women go to the tomb to anoint Jesus' body. They find the stone at the doorway rolled back and a young man dressed in white inside. The man says that Jesus has risen and tells them to inform the disciples. The women run away, terrified. Several encounters with the risen Jesus are described, including with Mary Magdalene and with the disciples. Jesus tells the disciples to go out and preach, and then ascends into heaven.

So then the Lord ... was received up into heaven. Mark 16:19

Resurrection of Christ

Raphael
1499–1502

In depictions of the resurrection in Renaissance art, Christ is often shown hovering mid-air above an open sarcophagus and holding a standard in his hand—a white flag with a red cross. This "Resurrection cross" symbolizes Christ's power and victory over death. The symbol originated in the 4th century from a vision by Constantine the Great, the first Roman emperor to convert to Christianity.

When the Sabbath was past, Mary Magdalene, and Mary the mother of James, and Salome, bought spices, that they might come and anoint him. **2** Very early on the first day of the week, they came to the tomb when the sun had risen. **3** They were saying among themselves, "Who will roll away the stone from the door of the tomb for us?" **4** for it was very big. Looking up, they saw that the stone was rolled back.

5 Entering into the tomb, they saw a young man sitting on the right side, dressed in a white robe, and they were amazed. **6** He said to them, "Don't be amazed. You seek Jesus, the Nazarene, who has been crucified. He has risen. He is not here. Behold, the place where they laid him! **7** But go, tell his disciples and Peter, 'He goes before you into Galilee. There you will see him, as he said to you.'"

8 They went out, and fled from the tomb, for trembling and astonishment had come on them. They said nothing to anyone; for they were afraid. [*The Gospel of Mark ends at verse 8 in some manuscripts.*] **9** Now when he had risen early on the first day of the week, he appeared first to Mary Magdalene, from whom he had cast out seven demons. **10** She went and told those who had been with him, as they mourned and wept. **11** When they heard that he was alive, and had been seen by her, they disbelieved. **12** After these things he was revealed in another form to two of them, as they walked, on their way into the country. **13** They went away and told it to the rest. They did not believe them, either.

14 Afterward he was revealed to the eleven themselves as they sat at the table, and he rebuked them for their unbelief and hardness of heart, because they did not believe those who had seen him after he had risen. **15** He said to them, "Go into all the world, and preach the Good News to the whole creation. **16** He who believes and is baptized will be saved; but he who disbelieves will be condemned. **17** These signs will accompany those who believe: in my name they will cast out demons; they will speak with new languages; **18** they will take up serpents; and if they drink any deadly thing, it will in no way hurt them; they will lay hands on the sick, and they will recover."

19 So then the Lord, after he had spoken to them, was received up into heaven, and sat down at the right hand of God. **20** They went out, and preached everywhere, the Lord working with them, and confirming the word by the signs that followed. Amen.

The Risen Christ Appears to Mary Magdalene

Fra Bartolomeo

c. 1506

According to Mark, Mary Magdalene was the first person to see the risen Christ. In the background of this scene the artist also depicts the resurrection (left) and the three women on the way to the tomb (right).

The Ascension

French School

15TH CENTURY

This scene from the *Life of Christ* fresco in the Chapel of
Saint-Sébastien in Lanslevillard, France, shows Jesus' disciples
witnessing the risen Christ ascending into heaven.

Scenes from the Life of Christ

Franz Mayer & Co.
1888

The East Window of the Church of St. Mary the Virgin in Long Crendon, England, shows several scenes from the life of Jesus as depicted in the Gospels. From left: the nativity (not mentioned in Mark's Gospel); the baptism of Jesus by John the Baptist; the crucifixion; the women at the tomb after the resurrection; and the ascension of the risen Christ into heaven.

INDEX

CREDITS

Quarto would like to acknowledge the following for supplying images reproduced in this book:

The Art Archive: British Museum/Harper Collins Publishers *page 6*; Thyssen Bornemisza Collection Madrid/Mondadori Portfolio/Electa *page 36*; A. Dagli Orti *page 42*

Alamy: Peter Horree *pages 10–11*; SuperStock *page 13*; The Art Gallery Collection *pages 16–17, 24–5 & 86–7*; PAINTING *pages 18–19*; The Art Archive *pages 26–7, 82–3, 90, 122 &123*; jozef sedmak *page 76*; Heritage Image Partnership Ltd *pages 106–7*; INTERFOTO *page 114*; Colin Underhill *pages 124–5*

The Bridgeman Art Library: Christie's Images *page 98*

Corbis Images: The Print Collector *page 2*; Fred de Noyelle/Godong *pages 14 & 31*; Brooklyn Museum *pages 32–3 & 64–5*; Burstein Collection *page 39*; Lebrecht Music & Arts *page 53*; Francis G. Mayer *page 62*; Alfredo Dagli Orti/The Art Archive *page 120*

Getty Images: De Agostini *pages 22, 48, 69, 94, 100–1, 104–5, 110–11 & 112*; SuperStock *pages 44–5, 56–7 & 70*; The Bridgeman Art Library *pages 50–1 & 115*; UIG *pages 58, 89 & 102*; Philippe Lissac *page 75*; Alinari *page 81*; Mondadori Portfolio *pages 116–17*

Shutterstock: jorisvo *page 1*; Ajay Shrivastava *page 3 (cross used throughout book)*; Keith McIntyre *page 4*; Nella *pages 4–7 & 126–8 (patterned background papers)*

All other photographs and illustrations are the copyright of Quarto Publishing plc. While every effort has been made to credit contributors, Quarto would like to apologize should there have been any errors or omissions—and would be pleased to make the appropriate correction for future editions of the book.